The SUPER CONFIDENCE Factor

The 5 Step Super Formula That Empowers You To Don Your Cape & FLY As The Authority You Truly Are!

www.SuperheroConfidence.com

Copyright © 2015-2018 Amanda Robins

All rights reserved. No part of this publication may be reproduced, stored in a retrieval system, or transmitted in any form, or by any means, electronic, mechanical, photocopying, recording or otherwise without the prior written permission of the author.

ISBN: 978-0-9875967-9-6

Limit of Liability/Disclaimer of Warranty: This book is for entertainment purposes only. The author and publisher do not warrant the performance, effectiveness or applicability of any of the methods within this book. The author and publisher shall in no event be held liable to any party for any direct, indirect, punitive, special, incidental or other consequential damages arising directly or indirectly from any use of this material, which is provided "as is", and without warranties.

For more information on Amanda Robins please visit www.AmandaRobins.com

"Be Prepared To Stave Off Any Confidence-Sucking Villains"

"It doesn't matter whether you take command of a room just by walking into it...or if you'd rather disappear into the floor rather than turning the spotlight on yourself. In her book 'Superhero Confidence,' Amanda Robins makes cranking up the volume on your inner superhero easy. The short exercises are profound, and they really work. And let's face it, at one time or another even Superman has a bad day. Be prepared to stave off any confidence-sucking villains by grabbing your copy of 'Superhero Confidence' now."

~ Lorrie Morgan-Ferrero www.RedHotCopy.com

"I Couldn't Stop Turning The Pages!"

"I've just sat and read Superhero Confidence by Amanda Robins & The Superfy Alliance - cover to cover in one go. This book had me digging deeper, thinking about how I could bring about the changes I need to take in what I can offer the world from ordinary to extraordinary.

I couldn't stop turning the pages! The book takes you on a journey to help you acknowledge your skills and how you can share them with others. Amanda's happiness and love for what she does shines through the words.

It's chock-a-block full of real stories from real people, including Amanda, the Superfy Alliance and other famous people about their success in business and in life. For me, this confirms and strengthens what Amanda has to say. Combined with the exercises in each chapter, this book helps you to discover yourself, your skills and what you can share. It's a treasure for anyone looking for their next steps to take them further! I'm off to buy a journal to start work on those exercises!"

~ Caroline Angell www.EarthAngellAuthor.com

"Entertaining and Actionable!"

"Amanda Robins and her Superfy Alliance have come together to write an entertaining and actionable book that is sure to inspire millions of women to unleash their highest potential and share it with the world! The book shows the steps that have helped hundreds of women to soar and shine. The candid stories that the Alliance shares generously are inspiring and connect with the reader in a powerful way. As Heather Barker put it, "Each and every day my confidence grows as I step into the leadership role I love." May we all feel that way about our own leadership journey!"
~Patrice Dunckley, Career Mentor

"This is the kind of book that comes along to save you"

"This is the kind of book that comes along to save you from repeating mistakes or undervaluing yourself in your life because of previous conditioning. As women, we are often told that we are only of value if we put everyone else first and ourselves last. We are told that if we self-sacrifice we will be good people. But, instead we end up burnt out, sick and no good to anybody. Amanda Robins and her contributors will tell you a different method for life success, a way to find personal growth and inner strength, without compromising your need to nurture your loved ones. If you are feeling overwhelmed by life and you need a change, I recommend you read Superhero Confidence, use the exercises and step out of the old way and into a new, brighter day."

~ Cat Edwards Spiritual Mentor, Clairvoyant, Civil Celebrant and Writer. www.catedwardsclairvoyant.com

"I Love It When The Right Book Drops Into Your Life"

"Divine intervention is what I'd like to declare this book! "Superhero Confidence: The 5 Step Formula To Strap On Your Cape To Fly As The Expert You Truly Are!" is life changing. I love it when the right book drops into your life at exactly the right time.

If you are reading this review, then this book is for you, right now! By following the step by step process, which is brilliantly laid out by author, Amanda Robins, you will be able to identify your individual recipe for personal fulfillment as well as financial abundance.

One of the basic ingredients of this recipe is to learn how to "FLY," as a Superhero, which Amanda defines as learning how to "Fully Love Yourself!" She goes on to say, on page 106, "Then when you feel this, (and) follow your passion and shine your natural brilliance throughout your work you will also Fully Love Your Business!" I believe that no matter where you are in your business (just starting out, or have been in business a long time) this book will help you take your natural born gifts to the next level. Don't delay, start reading today and fly like the Superhero you truly are."

~Lisa Jones, author and speaker
www.ArtofLivingHappy.com

"I Love The Fresh Writing Approach"

"I love the fresh writing approach which ultimately catches the attention of the reader. The authentic style is refreshing and breaks down the "illusion barrier". In dealing with many situations and people I find the subject of 'ego' is often brushed aside whereas now I understand its importance from Wayne Dyer and your book.

You really are a refreshing ideas person on a mission, who chunks down into bite sized pieces how to achieve the superhero dream - well done!"

~Michele Flynn http://about.me/micheleflynn

WHAT IS YOUR HERO ARCHETYPE?

TAKE THE TEST

Let me guess what you are thinking…

"Hero? Me?"

YES! YOU!

Inside each and every one of us is a hero with special heroic personality traits that when understood empower you to step up and FLY!

IN JUST THREE MINUTES YOU CAN DISCOVER YOUR HERO PERSONALITY & GAIN CLARITY ON THE POWER YOU HAVE!

To Find Your Hero Personality Archetype visit
http://askbrainstorm.com/test/

This book is dedicated to my family who have always believed in me even when I didn't believe in myself.

It is also dedicated to the Superfy Alliance. Each and every day they make my life better! The joy I get watching them FLY is worth every minute of work I put into the Superfy Universe! I am honoured to share this book filled with their stories.

Dedication

Table of Contents

Foreword ~ Pete Godfrey 12
Introduction 15
Chapter One ~ Are you ready to discover your superpowers? 20
    Superpowers? Really? 20
    Confidence vs Ego 21
    The Story Of Confidence 21
        Exercise: Ego Check 23
    Finding your inner child 24
    Butterfly Kisses 25
        Exercise: Reconnect With Your inner child 26
    Where do you begin? 26
    Your Origin Story 27
    10 Million Dollar Check 28
        Exercise: Uncover Your Origin Story 30
    Tell me your dreams 30
    Confidence, can it be bottled? ~ Lisa Suling-Maslin 32
        Exercise: What Is Your BIG Dream? 35
    Superhero Confidence Formula 36

Chapter Two ~ Escaping the Ordinary 38
    Where you born to be ordinary? 38
    Something Missing 38
    Too Bland For Who I Really Am ~ Claire Takács 40
        Exercise: Greatness List 42
    Ball and Chain 43
    Nails In The Fence 46
        Exercise: Cutting Off The Ball And Chain 47
    Lost in the crowd 47
        Exercise: Getting Started 50

Chapter Three ~ Embrace the Change 52
    Embodying The Superhero In You 52
    Has Anyone Seen My Brave Girl Jeans? ~ Megan Darcy 53
        Exercise: Identify Your Inner Super Hero 59

Working with your inner critic 59
It's What's Inside That Make It Fly! 60
    Exercise: What Is Your Inner Critic Telling You? 61
Addressing the haters 61
    Exercise: Understanding The Haters 64
Identifying Your Cheer Squad 64
I really do believe in magic and that anything IS possible ~
Heather Barker... 66
    Exercise: List Your Cheer Squad 68
Your Uniqueness... 69
Soul Surfer... 71
    Exercise: What Makes You Unique? 72
Your natural abilities 72
Made A Million, Lost A Million.. 75
    Exercise: Discover Your Natural Abilities................................75
Lean into the stretch 76

Chapter Four ~ Training your Superpowers 78
Let The Training Begin 78
    Exercise: Circle of Excellence..79
Moving Boulders 80
Puff out your chest 80
    Exercise: Fake It Until You Make It 81
Kryptonite 82
    Exercise: Kryptonite To Power 83
Archnemesis 84
The Fastest Woman On This Earth 85
    Exercise: Archnemesis 87
Creating Magic 87
Wow My Life Began To Change Fast! ~ Trudi Afford 90
    Exercise: Creating magic..93
Getting Knocked Down 94
Shake It Off and Step Up 95
    Exercise: Getting Knocked Down...96

Chapter Five ~ Don on your Cape 98
Time to Don on your Cape 98
Stepping into your Persona.. 98
Owning My Own Power ~ Sheila Kennedy 100

  Exercise: Step Into Your Persona 104
Soar above the Crowd **104**
  Exercise: Larger than life presence 107
Cape Flappers..**107**
Watching From Above..**109**
  Exercise: Cape Flapping 111
Behind Every Great Success **111**

Chapter Six ~ FLY 114
Confidence Takes Practice **114**
Your Vibe Attracts Your Tribe..**115**
  Exercise: Your Vibe 117
Super Sidekicks..**117**
  Exercise: Super Sidekicks 119
Superhero Alliance..**119**
From Self Employed Psychologist To 'Woman With A Mission' ~ Sallyanne Stone **121**
  Exercise: Superhero Alliance 125

Chapter Seven ~Putting It All Together 127
Now Comes The Fun Part!..**127**
The Little Things Matter...**127**
Putting the Superhero Confidence Formula Into Action **128**
  Are you ready to discover your superpowers? 128
  Step One: Escaping the Ordinary 129
  Step One: Escaping the Ordinary 129
  Step Three: Training your Superpowers 130
  Step Four: Don your Cape 131
  Step Five: FLY 132
"I Just Needed An Epic Failure to Spur Me On...." ~ Con Dolmas...**132**
Final Thoughts **139**
Meet Amanda...**140**

Foreword ~ Pete Godfrey

Do you ever get the feeling you haven't reached your full potential? That's there is more to you and your life? That you've settled?

If so, you are not alone. Millions of people around the world live lives of quiet desperation, as Thoreau so eloquently said all those years ago.

It's not your fault. We get caught up with life. Caught up with earning a living and doing the right thing. It doesn't leave us much time to find out who we really are and what we are really capable of achieving.

What's worse, most of us are told at an early age not to get too big for our boots. To be happy with what we've got. Not to rock the boat. The sad news is, many of us take this advice on board, and as we grow older, these thoughts become ingrained, effectively stopping us from living a full and wonderful life.

The good news is, it doesn't have to be this way. You can find your true calling. And you can live the life you secretly dream of.

The fact is, each one of us is special. We're unique. There is no one exactly like you anywhere on this planet. You have skills and ideas that could benefit so many others.

So if you've ever felt there is more to life, that maybe you're just 'going through the motions', and you want to finally find your true path, your true calling, then you've come across the right book at the right time.

That's because in her new book, 'Superhero Confidence', Amanda Robins gives you the skills, knowledge and confidence to step forward into a brighter, more rewarding future.

Together with the Superfy Alliance, they share their stories on how they overcame their fears and stepped into a whole new world brimming with confidence and overflowing with opportunities.

With heart-felt stories, practical advice, and unique exercises, this book shows you how to build your confidence, embrace your uniqueness, and how to share it with the world and become the superhero of your niche.

The only things stopping you from reaching your full potential is finding the right advice, and then taking action.

Amanda and The Superfy Alliance give you the tools to shine.

But it's up to you to take the next step.

I wish you well on your journey.

And if a guy like me who left school at 15 can become one of Australia's most respected and highest paid copywriters, I believe anyone can change their lives in an instant.

You just need to decide you want to change. And then figure out what you really want.

The stories, advice and exercises contained in this book give you the keys to unlocking your future.

I'm getting excited for you already.

Pete Godfrey
Wizard of Words
Copywriter & Sales Strategist
www.PeteGodfrey.com

Introduction

Once upon a time lived an undiscovered hero. Lost in a world of people who she thought were so much better than her. You see, she had a dream. A dream to help people, to provide a wonderful life for her family, to have a business that gave her options.

It was a dream that seemed so far out of reach. You see she bought into the magical spells and potions of online marketing. She wanted so badly to believe that it was so easy to make money by doing next to nothing. All the pictures of the holidays, cars, homes and piles of money just sucked her in. The pictures of the smiling successful people telling you how much money they made in such a short period of time sounded like the answer she was seeking.

So she invested. She scrimped and saved to learn these secrets of success. She learned, she followed the directions and implemented what was in these courses but they just didn't work. It was back to square one.

She blamed herself. "If only I had more money to invest in better programs, if only I could look all glamorous like these other experts, if only I could be someone else, someone better."

The thing that she was missing is that she was fantastic just as she was. She achieved success in the things she did. She had special and unique talents that somehow were overlooked as she chased the next bright shiny object that was going to give her what she wanted.

That's when she found people that enjoyed being in her company. People that believed in her and her talents. People who told her that she is worthy to be the expert!

Still the self-doubt and insecurities ran wild. "I'm too fat...I don't talk clearly enough... I have typos in my work... I'm not connected enough."

Then one day she took a step back. She stopped playing the comparison game and really looked into what she was good at.

What did she have to offer? What could she do that people wanted?

Not finding an immediate answer, she took a step back and ended up watching a lot of television. I mean a lot. After quite a few seasons of a superhero TV series she started to see a similarity between superheroes and business owners.

Then it hit her! She was going to become a superhero! Yes that's right "A Superhero!"

When she compared the traits of superheroes and entrepreneurs, she discovered that they were practically the same. This meant that she already was one - she just didn't know it yet.

Now what would she be called?

The search began. The search to dig deep into what she loved and what she was awesome at. What could that be? What was it that people loved her to do?

The answer was obvious. BRAINSTORM!!!

For the past 15 years the thing that people wanted to do with her and what she absolutely loved to do was brainstorm!

That is where the legend began.

With no idea of how she could find a way to build a business selling ideas, she strapped on her cape and started.

It was weird. As a superhero she was able to step outside of her plain old ordinary self and become something so much bigger and better. She could really show off her powers in a fun and exciting way. She could laugh at herself. She called herself "Brainstorm", had a cartoon avatar and decided to just run with it. In many places she would have been locked away in the looney bin but instead people embraced the concept.

In fact they loved it. It was freeing to be able to just be herself. To step up into her superhero persona and just have fun while creating something POWerful!

That undiscovered hero was me! Amanda Robins!

I am here to tell you that you too are an undiscovered hero. You have something POWerful in you just bursting to get out. You are ahhhh-mazing and the world needs you!

The best thing is you don't have to go full superhero like I did to really embrace your inner superhero. It doesn't matter whether you wear your cape on the outside for the world to see or under your power suit, you too can have superhero confidence.

You would never have guessed that so many adults would be over the moon at receiving their very own cape as part of the Superfy Alliance!

Let us show you how to become a superhero! This book is designed to take you from being stuck in the ordinary to embracing your AWESOMEness to FLY!

The Superfy Alliance share their stories to inspire you and show you that IT IS POSSIBLE! Each of them have a different background, style and story to tell just like you do.

This is the beginning of your superhero story and I'm honoured to be your guide on this journey.

Now is the time to don your cape and begin!

CHAPTER ONE

Are you ready to discover your superpowers?

Chapter One ~ Are you ready to discover your superpowers?

Superpowers? Really?

Yes, I'm serious. Inside of you is something special. Something you were born to do. Something that people need and something that you can learn to embrace and put to good use.

Sometimes it is easier to hide behind excuses. Excuses like "There is nothing really special about me" or "What could I honestly have that people will want?"

We have all been there. Stuck in fear and self-doubt. Hiding our light because we don't feel worthy enough to shine. Playing small because we don't want to stand out. Holding back our message because we feel that no one wants to hear it.

NO MORE! Now is your time to FLY!

Fully
Love
Yourself

"To love oneself is the beginning of a life-long romance."
~Oscar Wilde

Confidence vs Ego

Please don't mistake confidence with ego. These are two very different things.

When you have a big ego, you have an inflated opinion of yourself. You believe that you are the best thing since sliced bread and everyone else pales in comparison. You will often find that people with big egos like to put other people down to build themselves up.

However, confident people believe in themselves. They know they are good at what they do and there is a feeling of power you get from being in contact with them. They don't have a need to keep people down because they don't feel threatened by others. It is their sense of self assurance that draws people to them. They are happy to watch you find your confidence because they know that that is the energy they want to be surrounded by.

If you know you have put in the hard work, made the sacrifices and you are good, then there is nothing wrong with feeling confident in your abilities. You can be confident and grounded at the same time. When your ego kicks in and starts to take over, you are headed for a rude awakening! However, I have a feeling that if you are reading this book, you are truly awesome, and your confidence is just waiting to get out and your ego has been checked at the door.

The Story Of Confidence

Confidence and Self-Esteem were BFFs. They went everywhere together. If Confidence purchased a new dress, Self-Esteem bought one exactly the same. They were very close.

One day a new child came to their school. His name was Peer Pressure. His friend's name was Hateful Words. They decided to give Confidence a hard time. They continuously teased her. They forced her to do awful things. It was so awful that Confidence lost Self-Esteem as a buddy. When Self-Esteem desired to start a dance class, Confidence said they would be no good at it.

Then one day, Peer Pressure introduced Confidence to Doubt. His goal was to ruin Confidence, but Peer Pressure said he had to wait. Self Esteem couldn't understand what was wrong with Confidence. Confidence now kept company with Depression, Low Self-Esteem, and Overeating. They were all friends with Peer Pressure. Self-Esteem lost all her friends. She felt so bad about herself. She went to see her counsellor, Good Words. She told her how to communicate with Confidence. She introduced Self-Esteem to her daughter, Encouragement.

Encouragement and Self-Esteem went to save Confidence. Hopefully it wasn't too late.

They found Confidence in a daze. She wasn't a vibrant, happy young girl anymore. She had dark circles under her eyes and had gained so much weight from eating junk food that she couldn't move. Encouragement was shocked and Self-Esteem was so sad she cried. She begged Encouragement to help. Encouragement started to hug Confidence. She loved her and held her tight. She told her that she was still a beautiful young lady with alot going for her. She held Confidence so tightly that Self-Esteem thought she would break. Confidence started to cry. As she cried, Confidence suddenly began to smile brightly.

Peer Pressure and his friends tried to fight back against what Encouragement was doing. They tried as hard as they could, but they couldn't tear her from the arms of Confidence. Then Confidence started to speak.

"Go away, Peer Pressure. Get your friends and leave. You no longer have any control over me." Confidence was now glowing. She and her friends did whatever they could to make sure that Peer Pressure and his friends never bothered anyone in their school again.

You can find Encouragement in yourself. When you do, Self-Esteem and Confidence follow.

Exercise: Ego Check

How do you know if it is your ego or your confidence running the show?

Ask yourself:

Am I telling people I am better than others?
Do I feel the need to talk myself up to get business?
Am I pointing out the shortcomings of others?
Do people feel that I am speaking down to them?
Am I resistant to hear feedback about my business?
Do I feel out of alignment with my core values?

If you answer 'Yes' any of these questions, your ego is running the show. Take time to centre yourself again and come from a heart centred place.

Finding your inner child

Once upon a time, a long time ago, you were born confident. You knew what you wanted, and you knew how to get it. You believed anything was possible and you could do whatever you put your mind to.

Until...

People told you that you couldn't.
They told you no!
They told you to be realistic.
They told you that you would never get what you wanted.
They told you that it's too hard.

These were people you looked up to. People you loved and trusted. So you didn't question them. You took their word for it.

Then you began to tell yourself these things. You repeated them in your mind over and over again until they became a belief.

The years went by and you became a grown up. A serious professional adult who lost their sense of fun and adventure. The sense that anything is possible.

Until NOW...

That's right! It's time to reconnect with your inner child. The part of you who believes anything is possible. The core of you that believes you can be, do and have whatever you want.

It's time to have fun again. Life is meant to be lived and enjoyed! I am here to tell you that you can be you, have fun and still be an authority in your field.

Here is one of my favorite stories.

Butterfly Kisses

There is a lot to be learned from children. There is a story shared through the generations about a father and his three year old daughter.

One day, a father got really angry at his daughter for wasting a roll of gold wrapping paper. Money was tight at the time so the father punished the little girl for being wasteful.

Even though her father had punished her the day before, the little girl proudly presented the wrapped gift to daddy on Christmas morning. "Daddy, this is for you" she proudly said.

The father was taken back and a little embarrassed about his reaction the day before. As he opened the box he found that it was empty. Shocked and angry he yelled at his daughter. "Don't you know when you give someone a gift there is meant to be something more than just a wrapped box?"

With tears in her eyes the little girl looked at her father and replied "But Daddy, There is something in the box. I blew butterfly kisses in it all just for you"

The father burst into tears and begged for his daughter's forgiveness. From that day forth he kept that box next to his bed to remind him of the unconditional love his daughter had for him.

> **Exercise: Reconnect With Your inner child**
>
> When was the last time you did something fun for no reason?
>
> What did you enjoy doing as a child that you think you're too old for now?
>
> **1.** Make a list of things you enjoyed as a child and then set a date to do them again. Step away from your adult persona for a little while and just let your hair down and giggle again.
>
> What do you think is possible when you begin to play 'make believe' with your future?
>
> **2.** Tap into your inner child, think back to when you believed anything was possible and then write a list of what you want to achieve. Then every day, spend time living as if these things have come true.

Where do you begin?

We go forwards by going back. Sounds weird right? However, until you know where you have come from, how do you know where you are going?

Throughout your life you have built up an amazing utility belt of skills, resources and connections that will come together to reveal your superpowers. These are things that you may not even know about or have really given much thought to before.

But even more important than that is the story of how you have come to be where you are now.

Your Origin Story

Every superhero has an origin story. A story of where they came from. The story of why they have chosen the path they are on or how that path chose them.

This is the story of where your beliefs have come from. Why do you feel that you are an expert or more likely, why do you feel that you are **not** the expert?

Your origin story will give you an insight into why you think the way you do.

Why are you hiding your light?
Who do you want to help?
Where did it all come from?

Your origin story will connect you to your tribe. Your tribe consists of the people you attract into your business. The ones that not only want to work with you but the wonderful people you want to work with.

People want to do business with other real people. They want to relate to you. They want to see a reflection of themselves in you. You will stand out as a person who is where they want to be. They want to be able to see that you were once exactly where they are now. They want to feel like you really "get them". You understand where they are coming from. You are a shining example of where they can go.

Your origin story will do this. It will show your human side and build that trust factor you need so that you can nurture solid business relationships.

10 Million Dollar Check

When Jim Carrey was younger, he watched his father give up his dream of becoming a musician to take a safe job as an accountant. Then one day his father was laid off and it sent the whole family into a tailspin. Having to find work doing whatever it took, Jim, his father and siblings took jobs in a factory at night.

Jim would go to school during the day and then walk home to the big stone house next to the factory to report for an 8 hour shift as a janitor. He was mad at the world.

One day, he announced to his father that he was quitting school to work at the factory full time. He had gone from being a straight 'A' student to falling behind. So at the age of 15 he thought that the best future he could have was as a factory floor manager.

Seeing the toll it was taking on his once loving and happy family, Jim's father decided to leave the factory with his family and they all began to live in a VW camper van. It was there that the whole family regained their joy for life again. It was like a huge burden had been lifted off their shoulders.

Jim had a passion for comedy and his father didn't want to see his son give up on his dream like he had done all those years ago. Jim's father would drive him to comedy clubs to perform. While Jim was not an instant success - actually by most reports he bombed - he was determined to make it big.

When Jim was 17, he used all his savings to go to LA to appear on the Comedy Store. He soon realised that he was a little out of his depth so he retreated to Toronto to work on his act. Something amazing happened. Even though most people would have seen the move as a failure Jim used it to his advantage.

At the Yak Yak Club in Toronto the MC would introduce Carrey with the same joke: "Our next act just got back from the Comedy Store, in L.A. – where he had great seats". This gave Jim the drive to really nail his standup act, which mostly consisted of doing impressions.

Through a series of highs and lows he continued on his path to follow his dream. Even when he fell into a deep depression he held onto the dream. One night in 1990 Jim drove his old beat-up Toyota to the top of the hill overlooking LA. While sitting there, broke and disheartened, he decided to write himself a check for $10 million. On it, he wrote 'for acting services rendered'. He had no idea how he was going to make it happen but he believed it was possible. It was dated for Thanksgiving 1995. He stuck it in his wallet and went about creating his dream.

By 1995, Jim was on a roll. He had great success with movies, which included Ace Ventura, Pet Detective, The Mask and Liar, Liar which in total netted him $20 million.

He has gone on to leave a great legacy behind him, all because he believed in himself, put in the work to make it happen and continued, despite facing great obstacles.

Exercise: Uncover Your Origin Story

Write your origin story.

Include details about:
What your childhood was like.
The events that have helped shape you into who you are today.
The experiences you've had and lessons you have learnt.
Why you want to help people.
Where your passion came from.
The first time you discovered your superpowers.

Tell me your dreams

Now you know where you have come from where are you going?

What is your BIG dream? Yes, I said it - BIG dream!

It is time to stop reaching for small goals. OK, you need those too but I want you to tell me your BIG dreams. What is it you really want?

If you could not fail, what would you create? What is your ultimate intention?

I myself have fallen into the trap of dreaming big but then when it comes down to finding a way to make the dream come true, I just feel this overwhelming pressure in my chest. I find it hard to breathe and the whole thing just seems impossible so I second guess what I want and pick something else, something smaller.

Can I let you in on a secret? Lean in a little closer!

The truth is that everyone feels like this. It is your body's way of dealing with stepping outside your comfort zone. Your mind goes into overload because you feel overwhelmed.

Here's the thing. You don't have all the answers right now. I mean, if we did magically have all the answers right when we needed them we would have no use for Google!

There is good news though. If you set your intentions (not your goals, your intentions), your subconscious mind goes to work. It's like buying a new car. You have gone on a hunt for a new car and found the one you want.

Suddenly you start seeing cars exactly the same as yours everywhere you go. The same brand, same colour and sometimes even similar number plates.

Where did they all come from? Surely they didn't have a rush in the dealership where you bought your car. No, they didn't! Those cars were always there but your subconscious mind didn't know they were important to you before.

We take in millions of tiny pieces of information each and every day. If we truly realised just how much our brain processes everyday our heads would explode. To make sure this doesn't happen, our subconscious mind just picks out what is relevant.

This is what you are doing with your intentions. You are installing a program in your mind to pay attention to opportunities to make achieving your dream possible.

Put it out there without attachment and you will be amazed at what you attract!

Confidence, can it be bottled? ~ Lisa Suling-Maslin

It was back in 2003, when a big fat yellow book nearly stopped me dead in my tracks. It was lunch time at my office job and the seeds of a new idea were germinating in my mind. I had heard how enterprising people were setting up businesses freelancing online as Virtual Assistants, helping other entrepreneurs with the things that they didn't have time for. I had always loved technology and tinkering around with new software so this suited me down to the ground!

But it wasn't long before a niggling doubt set in. Surely there were already similar businesses in my home town offering 'office support services'? I hit upon the idea of checking the Yellow Pages to see if this was true. At that time, that big fat yellow book was still a popular source of directory listings, before everyone started turning to the internet!

To my dismay, there was a long list of businesses offering office support services and my confidence took a nose dive. A little voice said, there's no point in doing this, there's far too much 'competition' out there! However, I knew deep down that if I didn't go for it, I would feel like I'd let myself down and I'd always wonder "What if?" I also knew that when you're doing something for the first time, you never feel 100% confident, you just have to feel your way along.

I started going along to business networking events and just getting out there. It was a bit intimidating turning up to these events, business cards in hand, not knowing a soul. But it wasn't as scary as I thought it was going to be. The people were friendly and, even better, they were very receptive to what I was offering!

Before long, I was able to go part-time in my office job and pretty soon after that, I had enough ongoing clients to work from home full-time. I got clients through said networking events and also online, through my website.

As time went by, I expanded my skills by taking courses in website design and internet marketing and transitioned to becoming an Internet Marketing Specialist. If I ever felt lacking in confidence I reminded myself that I had really good skills and experience that were really valuable to others.

Emails started coming in through my website from aspiring freelancers, wanting to know how they could set up their own businesses working from home. I noticed that similar questions were being asked over and over again so I thought, "I wonder if I should put together a resource for people showing them how create their own freelance businesses?"

I wondered whether I knew enough but then I realised that I was being seen as an expert by those who were just starting out. That was enough to bolster my confidence and I went ahead and created an online program which turned out to be very successful!

Fast forward to today where I'm putting together an online course helping others how to create their own online programs.

So - confidence, can it be bottled? Of course not, but you can definitely increase your confidence by taking steps forward even if you're not feeling 100% confident, plus it's important to have faith in your skills and the value that you can give to others. Lastly, always remember that you are seen as the expert to those who are just a few steps behind you!

LISA'S BIO

Lisa Suling-Maslin, aka The Cyber Sorceress, is on a quest to cast away the confusion and overwhelm that many entrepreneurs encounter when it comes to creating online courses.

Whether it's deciding on a profitable topic, pulling all the good stuff out of your head into something that's actionable and digestible, getting your course online or attracting your ideal students to enrol, Lisa has the solution.

With 11 years experience as an online entrepreneur, Lisa can help you navigate each step of the online course creation process. Not only has Lisa created her own online courses which have helped people across the world, she has been the secret weapon beyond many successful online business owners just like you.

If you're a passionate and driven coach, consultant, public speaker, service provider or practitioner who is itching to share your knowledge with the world through an irresistible online course, contact Lisa at www.lisasulingmaslin.com. You can also get her free eBook "Course Creation Confusion: The 7 Biggest Blunders You Could Be Making With Your Online Course & How To Avoid Them" at www.teachvirtually.com/blunders"

Exercise: What Is Your BIG Dream?

Tell me what your BIG dream is. Tell me in as much detail as possible.

Make a Vision Board

A powerful tool that we use in our family are vision boards. They are very simple to make. What you do is get a big piece of cardboard and find pictures that represent all the things that you want to attract and achieve in your life.

You can cut out pictures from magazines, print out pictures you find online or what we did is found pictures and made them the size of an average photo and then got them printed in full colour. You then stick them on the cardboard and hang it in a place where you can see it on a regular basis.

It is really exciting to see what you can actually achieve in a year!

So far, we have uncovered your origin story, set your BIG intentions and reconnected with your inner child! Now let's have some more fun!

Superhero Confidence Formula

Step One: Escaping the Ordinary
Step Two: Embrace the Change
Step Three: Training your Superpowers
Step Four: Don your Cape
Step Five: FLY!

Let the superhero confidence in you emerge one spectacular step at a time!

CHAPTER TWO

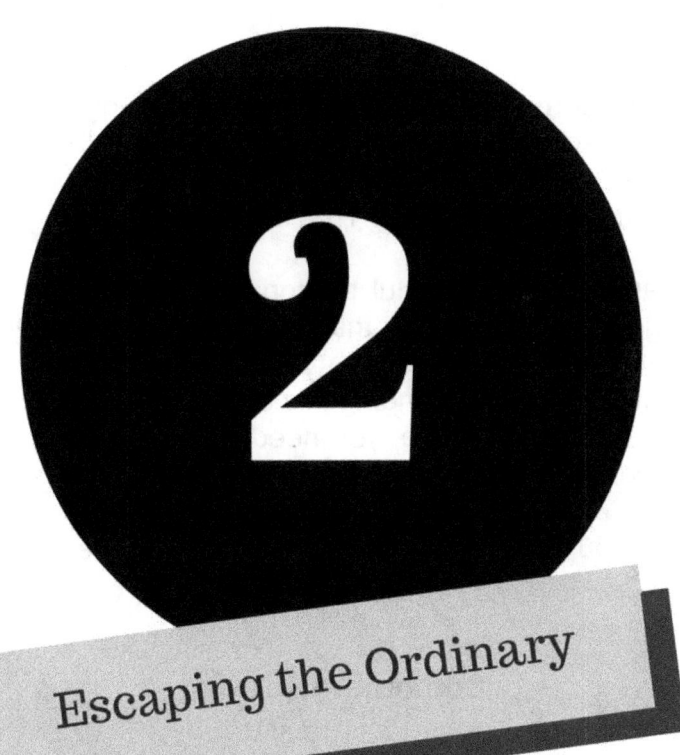

Escaping the Ordinary

Chapter Two ~ Escaping the Ordinary

Where you born to be ordinary?

There is only one answer to that.

NO!!!

You were born to be Extraordinary! That's right. You were born to be something special, but somewhere along the way you have been conditioned to not stand out. You've become afraid of being spectacular. That stops now.

You can be the wonderful person you want to be without making anyone feel 'less than' and honestly if they do, it usually has nothing to do with you. It is their issues, beliefs and thoughts that are bringing this up. For you to exist in your natural state of brilliance, you need to bring people up with you, lead by example and shine bright!

How do you really know your inner superhero is bursting to get out?

Something Missing

Have you ever felt like there was something missing? Something just didn't feel right when you began to move forward to success.

I mean, you were achieving things that other people were in awe of but somehow they were just unfulfilling. You couldn't put your finger on it. Yes, they were an achievement but they really didn't mean that much to you. It was just kinda blah.

You have this feeling that you were meant to do something great but you would never say that because people might think that you're full of yourself. There is just something in you that feels that you are meant to be so much more than what you are doing right now but there is this nagging voice in your head that keeps telling you "Who do you think you are? You are nothing special!"

No matter how much you try to hide it, there is that nagging feeling that something is missing. The feeling that you are meant to be GREAT!

I'm giving you permission to explore that now. You have permission to say "I am meant to do something great!" In fact, shout it out now! Say, "I am AWESOME!!!"

Woo hoo! Doesn't that feel good? Now let's back it up!

What great things are you destined to achieve? What is your intuition telling you?

Too Bland For Who I Really Am ~ Claire Takács

In late 2014, I left a well paid job to focus on building an online business, not really knowing exactly what it would be. All I knew was that I had so many ideas running around in my head and I wasn't sure how to make them link up and work together. I was also frustrated by the lack of role models specifically for women over 45 who are starting a business.

I had been provided withgiven a business idea by a successful internet marketer who had a 'formula' that was getting great results for their students. At first, I was really pleased that I had a tangible business idea to focus on. The trouble was, that idea and the formula was not quite 'me' and as time went on I became bored and uninterested with it. Other people close to me had noticed that the idea didn't reflect my personality and was too bland for who I really am. One of the positives of that experience was that I learned about podcasting and it rekindled a previous fantasy from a long time ago of having my own interview show.

I wanted to create a business that was fun and that I would be excited about everyday: a business that was built on my strengths and would allow me to indulge my passions of research and connection. Once I had a better idea of where I was headed, I joined Superfy.

The turning point was when I had a brainstorm session with Amanda (aka Brainstorm). We were able to work out ideas and ways to create a fun and varied business that I could build on my strengths, passions and, most importantly, my values. Three of my top five values are freedom, fun, and variety and now I am getting to play with these every day.

I am now getting to spend my days interviewing women from all over the world about their stories. These stories are the inspiration for other women to start making changes in their lives, changing their focus, their attitudes and mindset. I am so excited when I get off Skype after an interview, that I jump and dance around my lounge room like a little kid who has just met their favourite superhero.

My ideas and goals are now more focused and my days are full of movement towards my business becoming a reality. I'm making the most of opportunities to expand my comfort zone and get myself out there: learning to use different types of technology, and using my communication skills in a different environment. All the things I really love doing, like connecting with people, connecting them to other people and resources they want, doing research, interviewing women, getting to know them and their amazing life stories, and promoting these amazing women to the rest of the world. This is my dream.

None of this would have been possible if I didn't embrace my inner superhero. The world is my playground and I am going to enjoy every minute of freedom, fun and variety that comes my way.

Bio:

Claire Takács spent nearly 20 years both in Government and non-government sectors working with clients who had a multitude of complex problems. Claire quit her job in late 2014 to enjoy a temporary retirement and is now focused on establishing a business to support business women with information and inspiration to stop putting limits on their success. Claire has started a podcast promoting women who have started, or who are in the process of starting, their own businesses after the age of 45. Her websites are:

www.clairetakacs.com and www.clairetakacs.tv

Claire is a neuroscience geek and loves anything to do with the brain, the mind and how it works (or doesn't work, as sometimes is the case), and marketing. Claire qualified as a Life Coach with The Coaching Institute, Melbourne, graduating in 2009, and is a single mother of two and a grandmother of six.

Exercise: Greatness List

Make a list of great things that you feel you are destined to achieve.

Think BIG! What would you achieve in order to make the biggest difference in the world?

Ball and Chain

Now you have your 'greatness' list, what is keeping you chained down? What's stopping you from soaring to the heights of success you deserve?

It is all well and good to make lists, tell ourselves we are awesome and even believe it at our core, but somewhere along the line there is a force keeping us stuck to the ground.

This is partly because of our beliefs. What we think of ourselves, what we believe is possible and the obstacles we place in our own way to avoid things changing. These are all programmed in our mind. We will address these later in the book. All of these things can be changed with a bit of work. Like with everything, the more you use your powers the stronger they will get.

The other part of the force holding you down comes from outside of yourself. It comes from people and circumstances that you feel you have no control over. Let's face it, you can't control everything that goes on around you, however there is something you can control:

Your reaction to outside circumstances.

That's right. You have a choice. A choice about how you will react to the situation.

For example let's say someone does something that you believe is unethical. They not only hurt your feelings but they hurt your business reputation. Now you have a choice here.

You can a) go on a Facebook rant naming the person and publicly outing them to the world. Or you could do one of those passive aggressive posts where you cry "boo hoo, this happened, now feel sorry for me", while having a jab at an "unnamed" person, hoping that some people will guess who you are talking about.

Or b) you can rise above it. You can choose to sort it out directly with that person by expressing how you feel in a way that does not rip the other person to shreds. You are entitled to feel the way you do, but there is no need to hurt someone else just to make yourself feel better.

The first option happens all too often. While you may see a lot of people commenting on posts like these and feeding the beast, there will be people, ethical, kind and caring people, who see these posts and lose all respect for you. They will never tell you but they will be very wary of trusting you and they may fear that they will become the subject of one of these posts.

The second option however, gives everybody the chance to really open the communication. We are all human, we all make mistakes and if you deal with the situation with honesty and integrity, this will speak volumes for your character. People will trust you. You will attract people who feel safe sharing with you because they know that if there is a problem you have their back. Positive things will come out of bad situations, if you stay calm, really think before you react and rise above it all.

Can you see how we can choose what comes next by the way we deal with situations? If you stoop to the level of people around you that want to bring you down, you will stay chained to ground. But if you choose to follow your heart and live in integrity, then you will quickly rise above the challenges you face.

This goes not only for your entire life but also the business world. I know personally I'm so over people who believe you have to do whatever it takes to get ahead in business. Yes you will have to make some hard decisions and you will not please everyone, however you can run your business with respect and integrity.

In fact if your job is based on working with clients, the long term survival of your business depends on this. If you treat someone badly they won't work with you again and they'll tell everyone they come across about how you treated them. It is magnified in the modern technology age with the internet. If they don't like the way you treat them they will voice their opinions loud and clear.

The morale is, live and run your business with integrity and you will thrive!

"Our deepest fear is not that we are inadequate. Our deepest fear is that we are powerful beyond measure. It is our light, not our darkness, that most frightens us. We ask ourselves, 'Who am I to be brilliant, gorgeous, talented, fabulous?' Actually, who are you not to be?"
~Marianne Williamson

Nails In The Fence

There once was a little boy who had a bad temper. His Father gave him a bag of nails and told him that every time he lost his temper, he must hammer a nail into the back of the fence. The first day, the boy had driven 37 nails into the fence. Over the next few weeks, as he learned to control his anger, the number of nails hammered gradually dwindled down. He discovered it was easier to hold his temper than to drive those nails into the fence.

Finally the day came when the boy didn't lose his temper at all. He told his father about it and the father suggested that the boy now pull out one nail for each day that he was able to hold his temper. The days passed and the young boy was finally able to tell his father that all the nails were gone. The father took his son by the hand and led him to the fence.

He said, 'You've done well my son, but look at the holes in the fence. The fence will never be the same. When you say things in anger, they leave a scar just like this one. You can put a knife in a man and draw it out, but it won't matter how many times you say "I'm sorry", the wound is still there and a verbal wound is just as bad as a physical one.'

Exercise: Cutting Off The Ball And Chain

Get a piece of paper and draw a line down the middle of the page from top to bottom.

On the left hand side, write down all the things that are keeping you chained down.

On the right hand side, write down all the ways that you can come to understand these things and move forward in true superhero fashion.

Once the feelings around each list item change, cross them off one by one until you feel light and free from the drama.

"If we all did the things we are capable of doing, we would literally astound ourselves."
~Thomas Alva Edison

Lost in the crowd

Do you ever feel lost in the crowd? In the sea of business owners and self proclaimed experts begging for business, your powerful presence simply can't be seen by the people you know you can help. If only they could find you, you could show them just what you are capable of.

You are not alone. There are so many authentic business owners and real authorities buried deep within the market place. The real diamonds like you are hidden amongst all the useless rocks of the sadly mistaken people who believe that you can simply hang a sign up saying "Open for business". However, it takes a little more than that.

It takes someone like you. Someone who is kickass at what you do. Someone who is destined to be a real force of marvellous energy helping those who get a chance to work with you.

If only they could find you. If only they knew what you could do for them. If only you could rise above the crowd.

You can! One little step at a time. Let me show you how.

First, you have to let go of being "normal". You want to be extraordinary. You are not plain old vanilla!

We all get stuck trying to emulate others. You know what it's like, you see all the so called successful people and they all have the same look, the same words in their marketing, the same pose in their photos. Look at what happens when you try to be like them.

It's bad and I mean real bad. So you second guess your abilities again and again and again until one day, you find a way to be 'you' because 'you' is enough. Actually, being you is more than enough! You are AWESOME just the way you are. You can make your personality shine through in a professional way, just make sure that what you put out is quality!

Secondly, get out there. That's right - get moving forward. Start practicing, start putting your personality into what you do. Just start. Start slowly and find the direction you want to take.

I remember a little over a year ago, I had an idea for a book. This was going to be the basis for my business. I invited experts to be a part of it and they said yes. This was it. I was going to make the book a massive success and specialise in this. I wrote up a business plan, brainstormed products and services, and started a website.

Then it occurred to me that I didn't want to just focus on this alone so I changed direction slightly quite a few times until I decided to become a superhero. That was it.

I could make everyone a cartoon superhero for their business branding - that was the plan. I lined up artists, a website, packages and all the stuff I needed to deliver this service, however I was still just a little off the mark.

Not everyone wanted to be a cartoon character but what they did want was to access the power of being a superhero.

They loved being a part of the energy I brought to the table and they wanted to add the fun back into their business.

Now I get to help others with all kinds of things including marketing, book writing, brainstorming, branding, naming and whatever else anyone wants.

None of this would have been possible if I didn't make a start. And the book that started it all fits perfectly in with everything I do! Now it is just a matter of people telling me what they want and I deliver that rather than spending hours, weeks, months or even years making the perfect plan in my head.

Thirdly, be open to whatever comes your way. Joint ventures, mentors, clients or ideas, once you are moving forward, amazing things will show up. Be open to the possibilities but make sure they feel right before you take advantage of them, because you do have a choice.

> *"Inaction breeds doubt and fear. Action breeds confidence and courage. If you want to conquer fear, do not sit home and think about it. Go out and get busy."*
> *~Dale Carnegie*

Exercise: Getting Started

Make a list of things you can do right now to get started.

What action can you take today which will start you on the path to what you were born to do?

How can you begin to stand out from the crowd?

How will you know when you are making progress? What will that feel like?

Set a deadline to begin and make that public! You will be amazed at the response you get.

Are you ready to brush off the ordinary and be extraordinary?

Yes! Fantastic! Let's Embrace the Change!

CHAPTER THREE

Embrace the Change

Chapter Three ~ Embrace the Change

Embodying The Superhero In You

Your life is about to change. It may be very scary. For as much as we want to change, stepping into the unknown, even if it's for the better, is something we try to avoid. We try to keep things the same even though we are unhappy with how our life is turning out.

One of the ways we can begin to stretch outside of our comfort zone is by embodying the superhero within. You see, when we think of ourselves, we don't necessarily see anything special. We tend to undervalue what we have to offer because it is our stuff. It is hard to really see our self worth.

Here is the secret I have discovered since I decided to embody my inner superhero. When you embody your inner superhero, a magnified version of yourself, it is easier to follow your dreams.

It creates a way for you to feel powerful, a way to really tap into your brilliance without feeling like you are full of yourself. It helps you to be the real you because you are able to create a persona of someone who is confident, even if you don't feel that way. You can do the work that you love without a fear that you will fail. It even gives you a way to show off your flaws in a way that helps you to feel safe.

What is your inner superhero like? If you could amplify your best qualities what would they be?

Has Anyone Seen My Brave Girl Jeans? ~ Megan Darcy

Since becoming a superhero, it is not that I have become more confident, or at least that is not how I would put it, because a confident person is someone else. Someone I imagine as different to myself. Someone who is assured about their direction, decisions, and what they are doing. I, on the other hand can confidently say, am most assuredly not.

I am the someone who confesses their sorrows to a bowl of triple chocolate fudge ice cream, and somehow expects a solution to magically appear from within the delicious decadent over indulgent sweet sugary mind-numbing act of procrastination and a barrage of self-judgement.

I am the someone who will work for the price of a compliment, a quick coffee, or at the high end of my spectrum, a salted caramel pastry – anything as long as it is not cash. I mean, where would the usefulness in that be?

Oh my God! Once I actually worked for a cold bacon and egg McMuffin, even though I don't like and would never buy one for myself.

Yes, in other words, I am the expert who will work for free. How can I help you?

But most of all... Most of all I am the someone who wants to make a difference, knows they have something to offer, but cannot seem to pull their shit together no matter what.

However, the point is I am doing it anyway. Whatever "it" happens to be. Which is very different from where I was before I started this journey.

Well, some days I am doing it. While other days I am still falling apart at the seams like a cheap Gucci knock off.

I can't say for sure what prompted me to take Amanda's POW class in the first place.

Probably because it was free, full of promises, only three days long, and I had absolutely nothing to lose. After all, it wasn't as though business was thriving. No matter how well my intentions, or how in love with the vision I professed to be.

I mean there are thousands of these on the market, but what made this one different was the quality of the content.
There was something about it, which took my fancy.

Maybe it was those kick ass boots which Brainstorm is wearing, or her long flowing tresses. I mean who doesn't want hair like that.

But whatever it was, I knew I wanted to be a part of her posse.

For a start, it was not suggesting that I write sweet nothings to myself in lipstick on the mirror, in a bid to boost my self-esteem. Because of course, that is always the problem, right?

Umm, no!

I already knew I was fabulous. But I kept snagging my gorgeous one of a kind vintage gossamer lace sleeves on the details regarding how to explain and express said fabulousness to everybody else.

I mean, surely they should just know.

But apparently not.

Granted, it is still a work in progress, but it is looking far more stylish than the "desperately disempowered, don't really like it but it's all I've got, it doesn't really suit me, but surely if I gain another qualification, do another course, try a little harder, pretend a little more" ensemble I was previously trying to model on the runway of life.

But let us not go there.

My business acumen was good; I knew my market, and the issue I wanted to solve.

What's more, I knew how I wanted to solve it. So, what was the problem?

I was overwhelmed by the tiny details.

After all, revolutionising the way people who are blind, or vision impaired see themselves, and in turn are seen by others is a big job. And not a line of work for the faint at heart. I knew what I wanted to achieve, at least in essence, and I even had some idea of what that might look like. Or so I thought…

However, I was torn between doing what I wanted, and being loyal to the expectations of others.

What I realised was, I was spreading myself too thin, and therefore getting nothing done in any direction.

So, there was nothing else for it, but to give up the gum boots which were six sizes too big, put on my stilettos, pare back the business, rebrand, rewrite, and reorganise my life, and get on with being, well, fabulous.

And although I may not have everything perfectly in place, things are starting to gain momentum.

And wow, it's scary, crazy and exciting! Hold on - here we go, who knows where we'll end up on this ride!

I have gone from being utterly lost, ill focused, paralyzed with self-doubt, drowning in indecision, to "Well it doesn't have to be perfect, let's just get started, ok I think I can own this, and live".

I am polishing off my public speaking skills, presenting our product offerings in a public arena, accidentally writing a book, hoping to publish several others, potentially setting up a podcast, attempting to build a suite of websites, including an online shop, seriously considering a YouTube channel just for fun, and anything else which will allow me to buy more shoes, show off my new sunglasses, and contribute something meaningful to the world.

Between you and me, many of these things have a layer of complexity, which simultaneously terrifies and enthralls me. To be honest, I am outside my comfort zone, ridiculously under skilled and flying by the seat of my pretty little skirt right now.

But the point is I am doing it. And I absolutely love it.

But the biggy is - wait for it - I am asking for help.

I am no longer hiding in the back of my closet amongst my myriad of poorly manufactured excuses for why I cannot, should not, and will not do this.

Because the truth is, being an entrepreneur is a perilous life. There will always be mistakes to make, ideas to explore, risks to take, and rewards to reap.

So here's to my silvery sparkly tiara, warm soft sheepskin boots, "cannot live without you" mobile phone, unwavering sense of adventure, and willingness to completely fail. Because without that, success will remain an elusive golden bracelet, just out of a brave girl's reach.

MEGAN'S BIO

Megan Darcy is the Business Gypsy.

Megan is on a mission to encourage smart and sassy women to become more powerful and prosperous by seeing beyond the smoke and sparkle fancy branding, to the soul of a business.

Megan knows firsthand what it is like to achieve your dreams, no matter the circumstances, and believes everyone ought to have the opportunity to enjoy that same sense of fulfilment.

Among other things, Megan is an accomplished athlete, experienced speaker, writer, accessibility strategist, consultant, body work practitioner, and shoe shopper. But her latest venture is becoming a work at home mum.

Megan leverages her vast history in a variety of jobs, along with her cheeky sense of style and fun, to turn boring bland businesses into fashion savvy industry icons.

With her honesty, humour and occasional hijinks, Megan is able to look past the beautiful bling and busy banter, into the core of a business, and pinpoint its potential.

She has a particular passion for empowering people who are blind, and vision impaired to see themselves as strong, independent, and kick ass contributors to society, and in turn, be seen by others as just that. Megan is not shy about her disability and works hard to dispel the princess/pauper mythology.

This is why she is turning mobility and accessibility on its head, and transforming how people think, feel and act when it comes to their independence, options, and ambitions.

In her words, "It is not always about the blindy". She believes people ought to be known for who they are, rather than what they are not.

Megan is quietly creating a revolution of color, creativity, and candid conversations. So why not become a part of something bigger than who you are, what you have, or where you want to go?

If your business isn't quite matching your sense of style or just doesn't feel quite right, you need a "Business Reading" to see what the future of your business could hold. To book your very own "Business Reading" visit www.MeganDarcy.com

> **Exercise: Identify Your Inner Super Hero**
>
> What are your best qualities? What would they look like if they were magnified?
>
> What kind of superpowers do you have?
>
> What would your superhero name be?
>
> You never have to share this with the outside world. You can have a secret identity that no one knows about and that is just fine. Just create the superhero to step into and release your power.

"If you hear a voice within you say 'you cannot paint,' then by all means paint, and that voice will be silenced."
~Vincent Van Gogh

Working with your inner critic

We all have the nagging inner critic. You know that little voice that seems to butt in every time you start to move forward, every time you get an idea that you think would work or every time you just begin to feel good about yourself.

It is the little voice that questions everything you do. No matter how good you are or how much people tell you that you are amazing, there is still this little voice in your head criticising every little move you make.

You can however learn to work with this inner critic. How?

Talk to it. That's right. Why not learn to really listen and question your inner critic. While it may seem at first that your inner critic is there to hold you back, actually what it is trying to do is protect you. If you stay where you are in the plain old boring life you're living right now then you will be safe. You know this life, you know what comes next, good or bad, and you don't have to feel the discomfort of change.

Knowing this, you can begin to question your inner critic as to why it feels the need to tell you awful things. What is the belief system that is keeping you in the same position? Ask your inner critic and then listen for the answer. It may take a little bit of practice; however it will be well worth it. When you start to find the answers to your questions, you will need to recognise the beliefs you have to reprogram in order to move forward.

It's What's Inside That Make It Fly!

There is a story of a man who made his living selling balloons. This man had a great array of balloons in many different colours including blue, orange and green.

When business was slow the balloon seller would let a balloon filled with helium float up high so it could be seen across the entire park. Once the children saw the balloon floating in the sky, they would ask their parents for one and his business would pick up.

One day, a boy came up to the man and asked "If you released a black balloon would it still fly?"

Looking at the concern on the boy's face, the balloon seller gently replied "Son it is not the colour of the balloon that makes it fly, it's what's inside that makes it rise."

The same thing applies to our lives. It's what's inside that counts. That thing inside of us - our attitude.

Exercise: What Is Your Inner Critic Telling You?

Get a piece of paper and draw a line down the middle of the page from top to bottom.

On the left hand side, write down all the things that your inner critic is saying to you.

Ask your inner critic why it is telling you these things and listen for the answers.

On the right hand side write down the answers you hear. You will begin to see a pattern of what your inner critic is trying to tell you and why. Once you know why, you can begin to reprogram your mind and tell it that you are safe.

You can use tools such as hypnosis, EFT and affirmations to begin to reprogram your beliefs.

Addressing the haters

It is a sad fact of life that the more you start to rise up as the AWESOME person you are and begin to build on your success, the more people who want to pull you back down to their level.

As you begin to live the dream and reach your full potential, haters will come out of the woodwork. Now they don't hate you even if it may feel like that. What's actually happening is that they feel bad about where they are in their life. As they watch you achieve your goals, they begin to look at their own lives and see that it is not the way they want it to be. This is when they realise that it is much easier to pull you down to their level rather than look at themselves and do something about where they are.

The really sad thing is that these haters will often be people who you know and trust. People who you thought were your friends, family members who you believed would love to see you fly or even your spouse who vowed to be there for you for better or worse. Don't get me wrong, you will have strangers project these feelings on to you too but it will not hurt as much as the people you know.

How do you deal with the haters?

With understanding. Understanding of yourself and understanding of the person who is trying to pull you down.

You start with understanding yourself.

Ask yourself, "Why is what they are saying bothering me?"

If you are truly comfortable in your own abilities, what other people say shouldn't bother you because you know that it is not true. However, sometimes it can be that one little thing that they say that just touches a nerve. Why? Because it is an insecurity that maybe you didn't even know you had. It is like shining a blinding light on a flaw you are trying to hide so when someone points it out to you, you take it to heart. This is when you look for ways to overcome your insecurities and boost your self esteem so when these situations occur, you can deal with them quickly and move forward.

Next you start with understanding for the person who is hating on you.

Ask yourself "Why are they saying these things to me? What is that a reflection of in their life?"

For example, what if someone is telling you that your ego is getting too big and you don't deserve to charge your prices?

It can simply mean that they can't even imagine that what you are doing is possible. If you're feeling confident in what you do then chances are the problem is theirs. Instead of judging them, think of a time when you might have felt this way. A time when you might have given someone feedback that you thought was helpful but it hurt their feelings.

Now think of why you did that. Was it to hurt that person intentionally? Chances are it wasn't, so with that understanding of how you were feeling, give the same understanding to the person who is doing it to you.

It takes some practice, but when you have a true understanding of why people are doing and feeling a certain way and you can remember a time where you have made someone else feel the same way, you can basically mute the feelings. You are neutral about the situation and you can simply shake it off and move on.

> "You wouldn't worry so much about what others think of you if you realized how seldom they do."
> *~Eleanor Roosevelt*

Exercise: Understanding The Haters

Get a piece of paper and draw a line down the middle of the page from top to bottom.

On the left-hand side write down all the things that people have said to you that have hurt your feelings and affected your confidence.

On the right-hand side write down why these things bother you and what you can do to change these feelings.

Then get a new piece of paper and draw a line down the middle of the page from top to bottom.

On the left-hand side write down all the negative things that people have said about you that you know are not true.

On the right-hand side write down why you think they said these things. What issues could they be projecting onto you?

Now think of a time when you may have made someone feel like this and think of the reason you did this. Do you now have an understanding for the people who are causing you pain?

Identifying Your Cheer Squad

We so often pay attention to the people who are hating on us that we overlook the people who believe in us. They are the people who tell you how wonderfully you are doing, how they appreciate you and what you do, or who refer people to you because they know you will take care of them.

These people are out there singing your praises and are truly thrilled by your success. We all have them and sometimes we forget to thank them.

I know that each day in my business I get to be a cheerleader and I am also surrounded by cheerleaders. I hear stories of so many wonderful people who deserve great success, but they are held back because they don't have someone cheering them on. It breaks my heart seeing all that potential sitting on the shelf waiting to blossom.

When you begin to really pay attention to your cheer squad, your confidence will grow every day and you will begin to really step into your power.

I really do believe in magic and that anything IS possible ~ Heather Barker

My online journey began many years ago. One of my fondest memories of starting out was being in an online training group learning how to be a success online. We would all get into a hashtag group during the calls and excitedly say what we were learning and chime in, chatting to each other. There were quite a few of us in those days on Twitter, interacting at all times of the day and night, making friends and meeting some amazing people internationally. Because I like head hunting and interviewing people, it's easy for me to meet strangers and have a chat with them on Skype after we meet online, getting to know them quite quickly: what they know, where they are, what's important to them, how I might be able to help them through introducing them to people I know or programs I know about or gadgets that can help them. That's fun for me and easy.

So, all this time (it's been about 6-7 years now) I have been networking, learning, meeting people, buying their programs, joining groups, interacting and growing my connections on and off line. It wasn't until I started really appreciating the value of my connections, seeing how I can matchmake people and invite them to collaborate, that I cranked up my Heartwork Centre Community. It had been sitting unpublished on the laptop shelf of things to do, gathering dust. Recently I chose to don my cape, make it live and invite people to join together and collaborate in a truly Heart Centred Community committed to sharing, kindness, gifting and contributing to each other and having fun to boot.

As soon as I made it live, the group swelled to over 100 members overnight and has now steadied at about 220.

It is a community of play leaders, collaborators, those who have gratitude on their lips and hearts and who love to join in and meet others, hear their stories and be there for one another in life, work and play. I love to connect people with each other and have been doing this for years. Working with Amanda has given me what I needed to unlock my "Affinity Genie" as she dubbed me in her Unlock the Pow group, to truly step into what I enjoy and find a way to express and create that in the world.

I love to get to know everyone I meet in real life or online and help them work out a way to have their dreams become real. I love to help find a way and truly believe if you really want to do something enough there IS always a way. There is a way to find the support you need: both logistically and financially. That is how my "Genie" mind works, as I really do believe in magic and anything IS possible. Where there is a will there is a way.

Each and every day, my confidence grows as I step into the leadership role I love. It really is what HeARTwork is all about!

HEATHER'S BIO

HeartWork Heather is a Magical Genie on a mission to empower creative soul centered entrepreneurs to attract everything required to make a difference in the world.

Heather, often referred to as Hurricane due to her super-fast speed, takes you on a life changing whirlwind ride of self-discovery until you land exactly where you need to be.

She equips you with all the tools, connections, confidence and knowledge you need to bring your dream into reality.

Heather has gathered people and interviewed them, listened to their tales intently as a head hunting recruitment agent, therapist, coach, friend and colleague.

She loves to listen with the EARS of her HEART and get an awareness of what you stand for, what you wish to create in life and what you need to action it all.

Heather combines intuitive, creative, direct action suggestions to reconnect deeply with yourself, get clear on your path and make a plan of action. She will connect you with the people, information and gadgets you need to make everything possible.

If you are ready to work with someone who is 100% dedicated to being your cheerleader, mentor and advocate visit www.TheHeartworkCentre.com to connect with Heather.

Exercise: List Your Cheer Squad

You are surrounded by people who cheer you on.

Make a list of them and then send them a thank you note.

> "To be yourself in a world that is constantly trying to make you something else is the greatest accomplishment."
> *~Ralph Waldo Emerson*

Your Uniqueness

Has anyone told you how ahhh-mazing you are lately? Because you are!

You are a truly unique and wonderful person in so many ways even if you don't think so.

We often see our uniqueness as quirks. We are told that these are things that we must change in order to fit in. Who tells us this? The people who don't understand us.

You see, as we are growing up, we meet people who are different to us and have no understanding of us. We think that our upbringing is normal and that that is the way everyone's upbringings are. It is all we have known so we don't question it. Then we emerge into the world and we start to see people are different to us and we begin to question what we think is normal. Then as we continue to develop our understanding of the world we encounter people who try to help us fit in because they know what it is like to feel like an outcast and picked on. They were a little quirky when they were growing up and you can guarantee that someone made them feel that they were weird.

Here's the thing. What if instead of growing up thinking that you had to be the same as everyone else, someone told you that you could let your quirks out. They may need to be a little tamed but nevertheless they are a part of you. What if someone told you that some of your quirks were simply what made you unique? Would this have changed how you viewed yourself? I bet it would have.

Now that you are an adult and out in the big world, have you met people that are more like you? People that have the same interests, points of view and who share your sense of humour? I know I have and I love it.

It was a few years ago now that I realised that I didn't fit into what society thought was 'normal'. I was pregnant at 16 and by the time I was 19, I was single, raising two little boys. By society's standards I had thrown my life away and I was not going to amount to anything. However, I had other plans in mind. I had a belief in myself and I just knew that my circumstances didn't define me. It was up to me to lead by example for my boys. So I set to work. I studied from home while taking care of them. When my eldest son was in kindergarten I sat my HSC exams with all the other year 12 students that year. I was also working from home as a marketing manager for a local company, looking after my boys and putting my relationship with their dad, my childhood sweetheart, back on track. I knew that if I wanted something, I had to think outside the box and I did that year after year. I studied, implemented and just went for it. I tried for years to really find my place in the market. The place where I really stood out. Who would have thought that becoming a superhero was the secret all along? I am finally able to really embrace what makes me different. I own my quirks. I like them. I love interacting with people who think outside the box every day. I get to teach my boys that they have choices and that they are fantastic just the way they are, because I am living proof. I want that for you.

Tell me your quirks. Tell me what makes you unique. Tell me how you have a natural ability to do whatever it is that you do. Stop hiding behind the belief that there's nothing special about you, because I know that there is! If you can't see it, ask someone else because they will have seen something in you that you can't see. And if they can't uncover anything, come and see me. I will find it for you!

Soul Surfer

A while ago I was watching The Amazing Race with my youngest son, when Bethany Hamilton and her husband Adam competed. I was amazed at how Bethany took on challenges. She was climbing massive rocks, swimming, balancing trays and so many other things - and she did it all with one arm.

When Bethany was 13, she was spending the morning surfing alongside Tunnel's Beach, Kauai. As she lay on her surfboard with her left arm dangling in the water, a 14-foot tiger shark attacked her, severing her left arm just below the shoulder. Bethany was rushed to hospital for emergency surgery. Despite losing over 60% of her blood and suffering hypovolemic shock, Bethany pulled through with flying colors.

Despite the attack, Bethany was determined to return to surfing and just 3 weeks later she was back in the water.

After training herself to surf with just one arm, on January 10, 2004, she entered a major competition where she placed 5th. Since then she has gone on to compete in over 11 major competitions, placing in the top 3 a total of 7 times, including placing 1st 4 times.

Bethany wrote about her story in an autobiography titled *Soul Surfer: A True Story of Faith, Family, and Fighting to Get Back on the Board* which was later adapted in the movie Soul Sisters.

In my eyes, Bethany is a real-life superhero. She never let anything stand in her way and now she is not only an inspiration to people all over the world, she is a loving wife and very recently a mother.

Exercise: What Makes You Unique?

Write down a list of qualities that you have.

Make sure you include things like:

Your sense of humour
Your abilities
Your interests
Your favourite things
Your quirks

Then write down how each of these have served you in the past and how they could possibly serve you in the future.

Your natural abilities

You have special abilities that you may overlook. These are the things that come to you so easily, that you think everyone can do them. It seems so foreign to you that someone else will struggle with them.

During the school holidays, I taught my son how to build websites. It was literally a 20-minute lesson and away he went. I made a plan on the whiteboard for his own website and he just went for it.

Once he got the hang of it, I told him that we could set up a business for himself and his brother making websites for people. He turned to me with a strange look on his face and said, "Someone will pay me to do this?" I explained to him that what he thought was easy, some people really struggled with. It was a concept that was practically impossible for him to understand. He found it so easy and he couldn't understand that people would feel so overwhelmed by the situation.

This is how we can all be. We downplay our natural abilities because somewhere along the line we believe we have to work hard to get what we want. Then if it comes easily to us then somehow, we are cheating.

Have you ever completed a task and thought to yourself "That was too easy"? Then you start second guessing yourself and think you may have missed something.

This is what it is like to use your natural abilities. You are in your element and you are just having fun. You can't believe people are paying you to do this.
We all have something that we are really good at, yet we undervalue it, or we go into overthinking mode.

I did this. Can I tell you what my secret obsession is? Mastermind groups.

I have been in quite a few over the years and I love them. Do you want to know why? Because I got to do what I do best. I got to brainstorm. I got to connect with like-minded people looking to create wonderful things and I got to be a part of that. I would be like a kid in a candy store when someone would say "I have a problem". I would light up because I knew I was able to show off my superpowers. I remember someone in one of my groups said "I just tell Amanda my problem, then she goes quiet and you know the wheels are turning. Then she comes out with an idea that just hits the mark". I feel that I'm in my element!

Then the overthinking came in. "If only I could be paid to just think of ideas for people all day long, I would be in heaven". How on earth would I find people that would pay me to think of ideas for them? If you ever want to try something extremely hard, try selling ideas. So, I went on for years just using my superpowers to help people for free. It was hard, I saw people use my ideas to make a lot of money and I was getting really good at working for free. I can laugh about it now because it was so true but at the time it was so frustrating. Then one day I just got started. I put myself out there. I created a theme and a concept and just started charging for what I did. I began to value my abilities and amazingly so did other people. The thrill of that was addictive and I wanted other people to feel like this.

I want you to feel that thrill. The thrill of finding your natural abilities and then finding a way to make them profitable. You can get so caught up in needing to know the exact plan before you start. This can mean that you either don't get started or you blindly follow someone else's vision of what you should do.

You don't need to do that anymore. From this day forward, you can use your natural abilities to create a business that brings you joy every day.

Made A Million, Lost A Million

By his late twenties, Simon Cowell had made a million dollars and lost a million dollars. Cowell told The Daily Mail in 2012, "'I've had many failures. The biggest were at times when I believed my own hype. I'd had smaller failures, signing bands that didn't work, but my record company going bust, that was the first big one."

This didn't deter Simon, he picked himself up, dusted himself off and went on to become one of the biggest forces in reality television as judge for "Pop Idol," "The X Factor," "Britain's Got Talent" and "American Idol.". He now has an estimated net worth of $95 million.

Exercise: Discover Your Natural Abilities.

Make a list of the things you are really good at.

These are the things that you really enjoy doing. If you got the chance to do them on a regular basis and get paid for it, that would be a dream come true.

Make a list of ways you can use these natural abilities to help people.

Lean into the stretch

It can be a really weird feeling for someone to come along, tell you to let it all hang out and expose your quirks to the world because people will love you for it. To stop hiding your natural abilities because they are where the gold is (just wait until I tell you to don your cape!).

I felt weird when I first started doing this. I thought that my clients would think I'm nuts and I am sure there are people out there that do think I am absolutely crazy. However I can assure you that if you do it in a strategic way, it will pay off beyond your wildest dreams.

It will stretch your comfort zone but just lean into it. It feels scary yet exciting, strange but fun and then one day it becomes exhilarating. You finally feel free. Free from pretending, free from conforming and free from being normal.

Are you ready for that?

> *"Successful people have fear, successful people have doubts, and successful people have worries. They just don't let these feelings stop them."*
> *~T. Harv Eker*

Chapter Four

Training your Superpowers

Chapter Four ~ Training your Superpowers

Let The Training Begin

Are you starting to see just how powerful you are? I sure hope so because you are very powerful!

Now you realise that you have supernatural abilities, it is time to start your superhero training. It is time to start to really tap into what makes you special and use that brilliance every day in everything that you do.

I want to start with a little exercise called the Circle of Excellence.

Exercise: Circle of Excellence

Here is a simple technique to feel a sense of confidence whenever you may need it. It is a NLP exercise called, "Circle of Excellence".

Step 1: Imagine a large circle on the floor in front of you. It must be large enough for you to walk into.

Step 2: Now fill this circle with all the times you have felt confident. Think of a time you achieved something great. What feelings did it evoke in you? What colour are these feelings? Now in your mind's eye, take these feelings and put them into the circle. Repeat this over and over again until your circle is overflowing. (Your circle could be glowing. I like to see it as a bright sparkling gold colour).

Step 3: Step into the circle and let all those emotions flow through your body (I feel my body starting to glow, filled with bright shiny gold confidence).

Step 4: Take your circle with you everywhere you go. If you are presenting, put your circle on the floor and step into it before you take the stage. If you are writing, place the circle on your desk, or if you are just suffering from self doubt, put your circle on the floor and step into it to fill your body with confidence.

"Always remember you are braver than you believe, stronger than you seem, and smarter than you think."
~Christopher Robin

Moving Boulders

In ancient times, a King had a boulder placed on a roadway. Then he hid himself and watched to see if anyone would remove the huge rock. Some of the King's wealthiest merchants and courtiers came by and simply walked around it.

Many loudly blamed the King for not keeping the roads clear, but no one did anything about getting the stone out of the way. Then a peasant came along carrying a load of vegetables. Upon approaching the boulder, the peasant laid down his burden and tried to move the stone to the side of the road. After much pushing and straining, he finally succeeded. After the peasant picked up his load of vegetables, he noticed a purse lying in the road where the boulder had been. The purse contained many gold coins and a note from the King indicating that the gold was for the person who removed the boulder from the roadway.

The peasant learned what many of us never understand! Every obstacle presents an opportunity (to grow, or gain).

Puff out your chest

Have you heard of the expression "Fake it until you make it"? You probably have. Now I both agree and disagree with this saying. I believe that sometimes you need to fake your confidence until you really start to feel confident. Where I don't agree is when it comes to all these so called "experts" out there faking their way into your wallet. That's just plain wrong! Anyway, let's get back to the right way to use it.

As you're aware, we all suffer from self-doubt and second guessing. It's just human nature. Here's the thing, if we want to move past this we have to learn to play make believe and use our imagination until we really believe we are worthy of being great!

Do you remembering singing into your hairbrush as a kid or pretending you were a superhero when you were younger? I know I did. We used to believe anything was possible. Just because we didn't become a rock star doesn't mean that we can't keep using our imagination to create a picture of what we want. In fact, that is what will help us achieve it.

What I want you to do right now is close your eyes and create a picture in your mind of yourself. Now this is not just any version of you. This is the 'Super Powerful' version of you. With every breath, you are filling your body with more and more power. You can feel it pulsing through your entire body. It is empowering you to go out there and be your AWESOME self!

When you open your eyes, I want you to puff out your chest and get to work because it is up to you to make things happen! YOU CAN DO THIS! Can you feel it?

Exercise: Fake It Until You Make It

Make a list of ways you can boost your confidence in your abilities.

Make a list of ways you will know that you are doing a great job.

Kryptonite

Every great superhero has a form of kryptonite. If we were perfect, we would be so boring and that is bad for business. Why? Because people get bored with perfect. They want interesting, they want real and they know perfect isn't real. If you are out there promoting yourself as perfect, not only will people not relate to you, they will also think you're lying! Who wants to work with someone they don't trust?

Back in the 1930s when Superman first emerged, he was perfect. However, soon people started to become bored. I mean they could pretty much guess the story line. Something bad happened and Superman saved the day. There was no plot twist, he was invincible, and people got sick of it pretty quickly. This is when the writers introduced Kryptonite. This was the one thing that could stop Superman and all of a sudden, he could be beaten. People wanted to know if any of these bad guys could defeat him, so they kept reading.

This is what you have in your life. You have imperfections and flaws. I know, I'm not supposed to know of them but guess what. I DO!!! You have lots of them and they are wonderful. I can't stand those perfect stuck up people - give me real weirdos any day. I take people as they come, flaws and all. It's actually these things that help me relate to others.

The fact is, we all have something that has stopped us being the great leader we were born to be. Something that is holding us back from reaching our full potential. Something that we are afraid of people seeing. What is yours?

One of mine is typos. They plague me. I swear, some of the stuff I write makes me sound worse than a primary school child. Now I know that as a business professional this is not a good thing. I mean, I write books, blog articles, I chat on social media and I spend so much time writing sales copy and critiquing my client's work, it is crazy that I have typos, but they are there.

What do I do about them? One day I will hire a full-time proof-reader but until that time, I own them. I let people know. I tell them about my kryptonite and I try my best to proofread my work so that I put out something worthwhile.

The funniest thing is, when the autocorrect changes my words, the results are hilarious, but it is what it is. There is no point trying to hide it, they are pretty obvious, so I use them to my advantage, along with my other flaws. You can do this too.

What flaws do you have that other people will relate to? How can you work that into your marketing? How will you **own** your flaws?

Exercise: Kryptonite To Power

Make a list of your flaws.

Make a list of ways to turn these into positives.

"If you are insecure, guess what? The rest of the world is, too. Do not overestimate the competition and underestimate yourself. You are better than you think."
~T. Harv Eker

Archnemesis

Who is your archnemesis? Ok, so you are thinking I'm crazy but there is always something that you will be constantly fighting against. It is the reality of life. These are different to haters. What an archnemesis is, is the constant struggle you face in your business and your life.

Your biggest archnemesis will more than likely be yourself. Yes that's right, you will be struggling with yourself on your way to success. We all have a habit of getting in our own way, no matter how much we want something.

Other archnemeses come from outside forces. For example, one of mine, as you may have guessed already, are all these people out there claiming to be experts and having all the answers only to leave people broke and completely disheartened with themselves. They are the ones that are good at the sale but are completely crap at delivering the value.

Why are they my archnemesis? For two reasons. Firstly, all the money, time and effort I have spent trying to get their systems to work, to no avail. They promised the world but somehow it was my fault when it didn't work. To make it work, I had to keep giving them more and more money. I would wind up feeling disheartened and stupid. Stupid for not making it work or stupid for being so gullible.

The second reason is because I see so many people out there feeling the same way as I did. It makes my work so much more important and harder at the same time. I see people investing in these programs that simply don't work or they have been given a direction that is completely wrong for them. I want to help but the problem is, they have already invested all they had in these programs. They can't afford to work with the people that will really help them, and they just feel like it is impossible. It really breaks my heart.

How do you overcome your archnemesis? You lead by example. Don't get sucked down into the blame game like so many people do. What you do is rise above and really superfy what you do. You have something special to offer and people will begin to see that in you. If you are bitching and moaning, you are giving your power away.

Try this. Get a partner and stand with one person facing forward and the other person standing next to them facing them. The person facing forward holds their arm out straight and the person next to them places two fingers on their arm at the wrist. The person using the two fingers needs to apply light pressure in a downward direction and the person with their arm out resists at the same time. Here is how it works. Firstly, think of something that makes you happy. Think of what it is like to be using your natural abilities and how much you love that. Can you resist the downward pressure? Yes! Now think of your archnemesis. The person that really ticks you off. Can you resist the pressure? No!

Why? Because you gave them your power! That is what happens when you start to think negative thoughts and allow people to get inside your head. Next time you find yourself allowing your archnemesis to fill your thoughts, take back your power!

The Fastest Woman On This Earth

Wilma Rudolph was born in Tennessee into a poor home. When she was four, she developed double pneumonia with scarlet fever. This was usually a deadly combination but Wilma survived although she was left paralyzed with polio. The doctor though her that she would have to wear a brace and never walk again. Her mother had other ideas. She encouraged her to use her God-given ability, persistence and faith, because if she did, she could do anything she wanted.

Wilma said, "I want to be the fastest woman on the track on this earth." Against the doctor's advice, when Wilma was nine she removed her brace and took the first step that she had once been told would never happen. At 13, she competed in her first race and came way, way last. Then she entered her second, third and fourth race. She came way last but she didn't give up. Then came the day that she finished first. At the age of 15, she went to Tennessee State University where she met a coach by the name of Ed Temple.

She announced, "I want to be the fastest woman on the track on this earth." Temple said, "With your spirit, nobody can stop you and besides, I will help you."

The day came when Wilma was to compete at the Olympics, matched with the best of the best. Wilma was competing against a woman named Jutta Heine who had never been beaten. The first event was the 100 m race. Wilma beat Jutta Heine and won her first gold medal.

The second event was the 200 m race. Wilma beat Jutta a second time to win her second gold medal. The third event was the 400 m relay. She was racing Jutta one last time. In the relay, the fastest person always runs the last lap and they both anchored their teams. The first three people ran and exchanged the baton easily. When it came to Wilma's turn, she dropped the baton. But Wilma saw Jutta shoot up at the other end. She picked the baton, ran like a machine to beat Jutta for a third time and won her third gold medal.

It became history: That a formerly paralyzed woman became the fastest woman on this earth at the 1960 Olympics.

Exercise: Archnemesis

Who is your archnemesis and how will you reclaim your power?

Write this down every time you come across someone or something that is standing in your way, including yourself (we all get in our own way sometimes).

Creating Magic

It's time to start creating some magic! You know your natural abilities, you can see just how special you really are and now it is time to start putting all that into action.

When was the last time you got to use your superpowers? Who was the last person you helped?

"Hold on a second!", I hear you saying. "I have not helped anyone, and I am still not sure I have superpowers".

That is understandable, but I assure you that you do have superpowers and you have helped someone. You just might not have known it. Stop for a minute and think back. Someone has come to you in the past with a problem. They have a question that they know you can help with. They have come in a state of confusion, dismay or they were pretending everything was ok but you could see beneath all of that. Your superpowers just kicked in and you flew in to save them from their dilemma. It was just something so simple to you that you don't even register it as something special, however the person you helped thought it was amazing. That's right, they thought you were their hero. They came lost and left uplifted.

Can you think of a time like that? Yes! That's fantastic.

Now can you create that magic more often? Can you help more people with your superpowers? Even better, can you get paid for it?

It may seem like an impossible task right now, but it is possible. First you have to get started by getting comfortable using your superpowers. You need to feel that you're kickass doing what you love. You need to have proof that you can deliver. You do this by getting out there and practicing.

Then when you can see that you can deliver value it is time to start charging for what you do. It doesn't have to be a lot to start with. The point of this exercise is not the dollar amount but the fact that not only are you willing to charge for what you have to offer but that people are willing to pay for it. Then you deliver value again, the more the better. You continue doing this, growing in confidence of your abilities each and every time you use them. As your confidence increases, your superpowers become stronger and you raise your prices until you are at a point that feels right. The point where you know you can still deliver more value than they are paying for you to work with them.

Many people fall into the trap of going out there full force, charging crazy high prices because they believe that that is the way to go. They grow their businesses so fast only to find they are out of their depth or they don't really like what they are doing. Don't get me wrong, there is nothing wrong with moving fast but you have to really feel comfortable charging for what you do. One of the most awkward parts of running your business is asking for money. It is up to you to set your price, however if you feel certain you can deliver the value then go with a healthy price tag. If you are unsure that will also come across.

Always remember you are exactly where you need to be right now. All the things you have learnt throughout your life will come together exactly when you need them, in a way that helps you to live your purpose. It may feel like it is taking forever but you will make it one little baby step at a time. You are doing a marvellous job and as long as you are taking action every day, you are getting closer to where you want to be.

> *"Twenty years from now you will be more disappointed by the things you didn't do than by the ones you did do. So throw off the bowlines. Sail away from the safe harbor. Catch the trade winds in your sail. Explore. Dream. Discover."*
> **~Mark Twain**

Wow My Life Began To Change Fast! ~ Trudi Afford

When you've been doing Personal Development for as long as I have, you know that most of your thoughts and your actions come from your childhood programming. All that was said to you and all of the observations you made in your environment from birth to 7 years old, were innocently downloaded into your subconscious and form the basis of your belief system. This determines how you react to life and interpret the world around you.

It's hard to believe, isn't it? But it's true.

I have gone about my daily business for years, knowing this but never understanding how my own programming was holding me back from living the life of my dreams, delivering online courses, writing a book and speaking.

Over the years I've used many different techniques to try to impact my subconscious, knowing that it was under my control.

You know what it's like when you have big dreams and a vision of something that you want to do but that little voice in your head gives you a million reasons why it won't work or why you can't have it.

No matter how much I indulged myself in self-analysis, I had never been able to find the answer to what was stopping me from having epic success.

Sure, I've had success in my life in management positions, owning my own Travel Agency, writing and performing a children's CD, speaking, coaching and delivering training, but I've never had huge success that made my heart sing with gusto.

So how did things change for me?

Well, there were a couple of things that helped me to find the answers I needed.

Firstly, I started with a plan and I set new goals and time frames so that I had something to work towards. I knew that to be successful in a big way I had to follow the lead of highly successful people so I started emulating the way they worked and the systems they used to build huge success in their businesses.

Then I knew I had to surround myself with like-minded individuals and be held accountable. That's why I joined the Superfy Alliance.

Suddenly I was surrounded by a group of entrepreneurs who are passionately working on their businesses and that gave me the boost I needed.

Shortly after I joined Superfy, my husband and I went on a holiday to Vietnam.

I'd taken some work with me on the plane so that I could keeping working on my business, but I wasn't prepared for the creativity and inspiration that would flow through me while I was 35,000 ft up in the air wafting around in the clouds.

A nagging voice popped into my head telling me that I already had all that I needed to program my beliefs to have huge success.

Little did I know that I was about to develop a technique called the "Belief Transformation Technique", or BTT for short, which has a cognitive approach followed by a crossover tapping technique.

With BTT you uncover the beliefs holding you back and then program new beliefs that will help you to build the life of your dreams. Dowsing is also used to check if the new belief has been hardwired.

Transformation Statements I started using included:

- "I am energized and flowing with creative ideas"
- "I am confident and in flow with abundance"
- "It is safe for me to live the life of my dreams"
- "I allow my visions and my dreams to become a reality"
- "It's okay for me to be myself"

Wow, my life began to change fast!

I began to really implement what I had learnt over the years and as I embraced my inner superhero I found myself taking on tasks that once I would have put on the back burner.

There is an inner urge that exists within me now and things that I would have put in the too hard basket are now wonderful and exciting challenges.

My life is now full of exciting opportunities. I can now feel the fear and reprogram myself to fly.

Can you imagine how your life would change if your

subconscious was now operating on productive beliefs?

TRUDI'S BIO

Trudi Afford is a Belief Building Strategist and Coach and is the creator of the Belief Transformation Technique. Trudi empowers business owners, coaches, entrepreneurs and big vision holders who choose to step down from the ladder of fear to embrace their power and create the abundant life they deserve. Trudi Afford is the real deal. Armed with passion and kindness, Trudi helps her clients build new beliefs, new perspectives and new hope as they follow their hearts to massive heights of success.

www.trudiafford.com

Exercise: Creating magic

Make a list of products and services you can offer right now to start creating the magic.

What can you offer that people want?

Who can you help right now?

What can you do that will help you test out an idea you have?

Make a plan to get started and begin to move forward. Test, test, test and then see if you are onto something or if you need to go back to the drawing board. All that matters is that you are moving forward and paying attention to what is and isn't working.

Getting Knocked Down

No matter how good you are or how confident you may be, you will face times where you will fall on your butt. You will be going along, happily enjoying what you are doing and picking up steam and then suddenly you are dealt with a blow that stops you in your tracks.

It is at this point that you find out what you are really made of. It is when we are faced with a challenge that the real superhero in us comes out swinging.

One of the things I tell my clients is when everything goes wrong, get excited because there is something wonderful around the corner. Have you ever noticed that right before you are about to achieve something big, everything seems to go wrong?

You were cruising along nicely, and everything was falling into place and then BAM, out of nowhere, things just turn to crap. This is the point where many people simply give up. They see it as a sign that it was not meant to be. Other people however, see it as the last hurdle they have to jump to reach something spectacular on the other side.

It's like having a baby. You go through the worst pain you will ever experience in your life to get this beautiful gift. Once you hold that baby in your arms you forget just how painful it was to bring them into the world (it comes back to you pretty quickly when you find yourself in the same position but by then it's too late to change your mind!). This is what it's like with most of the big achievements you will have in your life.

The good news is, you can fight back! You can dust yourself off and keep stepping up! No matter how many times you get knocked down, as long as you get up just one more time, you are winning!

Shake It Off and Step Up

A parable is told of a farmer who owned an old mule. The mule fell into the farmer's well. The farmer heard the mule braying - or whatever mules do when they fall into wells. After carefully assessing the situation, the farmer sympathized with the mule, but decided that neither the mule nor the well was worth the trouble of saving.

Instead, he called his neighbors together and told them what had happened and enlisted them to help haul dirt to bury the old mule in the well and put him out of his misery.

Initially, the old mule was hysterical! But as the farmer and his neighbors continued shoveling and the dirt hit his back... a thought struck him. It suddenly dawned on him that every time a shovel load of dirt landed on his back... HE SHOULD SHAKE IT OFF AND STEP UP!

This he did, blow after blow. "Shake it off and step up...shake it off and step up...shake it off and step up!" he repeated to encourage himself.

No matter how painful the blows, or distressing the situation seemed, the old mule fought the panic and just kept right on SHAKING IT OFF AND STEPPING UP!

You're right! It wasn't long before the old mule, battered and exhausted, STEPPED TRIUMPHANTLY OVER THE WALL OF THAT WELL! What seemed like it would bury him, actually blessed him... all because of the manner in which he handled his adversity.

THAT'S LIFE! If we face our problems and respond to them positively, and refuse to give in to panic, bitterness, or self-pity, THE ADVERSITIES THAT COME ALONG TO BURY US USUALLY HAVE WITHIN THEM THE POTENTIAL TO BENEFIT AND BLESS US! Remember that FORGIVENESS-FAITH-PRAYER-PRAISE and HOPE... all are excellent ways to "SHAKE IT OFF AND STEP UP" out of the wells in which we find ourselves!

Exercise: Getting Knocked Down

Make a list of the times when you were faced with setbacks and then describe what you did to come back from them. What lessons did you learn?

Then make a list of things you can do to continue to move forward when you are faced with challenges in the future.

Use your superpowers and feel yourself get stronger each and every time!

> *"You have brains in your head. You have feet in your shoes. You can steer yourself in any direction you choose. You're on your own. And you know what you know. You are the guy who'll decide where to go."*
> **~Dr. Seuss**

Chapter Five

Don your Cape

Chapter Five ~ Don on your Cape

Time to Don on your Cape

Yes, it's time! Time to don your cape!

Time is really step up into your AWESOMEness!

Why would you Don your cape? I mean, not all superheroes have capes. Think back to when you were a kid. How did you dress up as a superhero? You put on a cape. You ran around with it flapping in the wind. You twirled and ran faster so it would move. Everyone knew what you were as soon as they saw you. You were a superhero!

I have to tell you that the excitement of strapping on a cape doesn't wear off. As part of joining the Superfy Alliance, our superheroes get their very own custom Superfy capes and they are super fun! The joy I get seeing all the excited photos and videos of them unwrapping their capes is amazing.

So whether you have an actual cape or it is just a symbolic one, it is time to strap it on and really BE the superhero you are!

Stepping into your Persona

Can you feel your powers growing as you begin to use them? Are the people you are helping to begin to really see just how awesome you are? Can you see new opportunities open up as you begin to really step into your element?

Now you are beginning to see what can happen as you start to get out there and really do what you were born to do, you can really feel what it's like to be a superhero. Each day you wake up looking forward to helping someone. You are surrounded by people who appreciate what you do for them and they just want more. They want to work with you more and more because your excitement and energy are addictive.

If you are not feeling like this, that's ok too. You may simply need to change direction slightly. The most important thing is that you are moving forward. Think about it. If you are taking steps forward, you can change your direction but if you are standing still, the only thing you can do is go around in circles.

No matter how you are feeling right now, everything you are doing is leaving clues as to where you need to go next. There will be things you love about what you do and things you could do without. For the things you could do without, can you outsource them or are they really not something you want to deal with?

If you can outsource, go for it. The little bit of expense is far outweighed by what you can do with your time. If you just don't want to deal with that aspect, try to find a way to get rid of it. You see, we can fall into habits of chasing the money rather than chasing the passion.

We have been taught to follow the money. To do what it takes to make a profit. The problem is that after a while the money never seems enough for putting up with clients that drive you crazy and having to do work that you have begun to despise.

What will really light you up is doing something you enjoy, something that you would do for free and then when you get paid, especially when you are a highly paid expert, it is a big bonus. You wake up looking forward to beginning your work day. The thrill of seeing your clients get results they never thought possible and being able to have a lifestyle that you are in control of, is something you deserve.

Life is much too short to spend it living out someone else's vision of what they think you should be doing. You and only you know what will make you happy. You deserve the chance to use your natural abilities and create something truly special.

Once you begin to see what's possible, that's when you need to really step into your persona to have the courage it takes to journey into the unknown. You will be entering a strange universe where anything is possible, and you will be flying without a net. It is scary and exhilarating all at the same time.

Owning My Own Power ~ Sheila Kennedy

I have often been heard to say that the universe moves in mysterious ways, or that when the student is ready the teacher appears.

I have been a holistic practitioner for around two thirds of my life, and while I am very good at creating an amazing foundation of knowledge and expertise, what I wasn't good at was being able to present and share that knowledge with other people.

I simply wasn't a marketer, nor even a faint shadow of one. I was very comfortable in my 'creative niche' and anything outside of that basically went into the too hard basket, or was put aside in the 'another day' folder. Besides, I felt that what I offered would probably appeal to a limited market and wasn't really 'saleable' to the public in general. My mind created fear, or "false expectations appearing real"!

Then I asked myself, what is the legacy you are going to leave for the world? How will people know what you do and how amazing it is, if you are not prepared to get out of your own way and share it with more than a select few?

These were tough questions and I really had to think about them seriously. How could I share what I did to a wider audience if I didn't step out of my comfort zone? Were people going to find me on my mountain top by spying a light as they flew over? Shouldn't I be considering who I could serve next on my journey to help people heal themselves?

Ok, so it was time to embrace change; what could I do to make a difference? To begin, I could be more aware and open minded to the advice of others, and that's when my life changed!

How? I saw a catchy description as a way to market myself by owning my own power, of really having the confidence and strong personality to OWN my true power, and a reminder that I owed it to my clients to help them. I owed it to the people that I already have and will inspire. And most of all, I owed it to myself. I took the challenge, and I stepped forward!

So, who am I and why do I do what I do?

My name is Sheila Kennedy. I am first and foremost a mother, grandmother and great grandmother, and it was my journey as a mother that led me to be the person that I am today.

Growing up in a medical family and struggling with ill health for much of my life, I saw some of my children walking the same path. However, for them the issues were exacerbated by learning difficulties as well and the options offered were in my mind undesirable.

Why would I agree to my twelve-year-old son being locked away in a children's psychiatric unit for an unspecified period of time and not allowed visitors whilst he was under such 'observation'? Surely society was failing him as it had me, and there had to be another way. If there weren't going to be any answers then I needed to create my own, and my journey of exploration began. As I searched for answers I met people who thought outside the box and along the way I created my own programs and shared them with others who were looking also.

Many years later, working with children is still a passion of mine, as is my belief that if you can help a child then you do not have an adult with a problem.

SHEILA'S BIO

Sheila Kennedy offers unique solutions to every day issues. As a holistic health facilitator, Sheila draws on many years of research and clinical practice to assist you to make changes in your life.

Sheila can help you, whether you are looking for an answer to your anxiety or depression, have specific health issues or learning difficulties, or simply know that there is more available if only you could find it.

Sheila's own ill health and search for answers to assist her children started her on a journey of discovery, not just looking for answers, but of wanting to create solutions as well.

As a Spiritual and Metaphysical facilitator and Vibrational Kinesiologist utilizing the unique "Sounds from Source" programs, Sheila is able to assist you in identifying your issues and healing yourself.

Many people credit Sheila Kennedy's programs with their return to health and wellbeing and of shining a light for a brighter future for their children.

If you are looking for more for yourself and your family, please contact Sheila Kennedy at www.soundsfromsource.com.

"To be yourself in a world that is constantly trying to make you something else is the greatest accomplishment."
~Ralph Waldo Emerson

> **Exercise: Step Into Your Persona**
>
> Before you tackle something that you feel nervous or unsure about, try this little exercise.
>
> Stand in a place where there is room to step forward without bumping into anything. Then close your eyes and picture your superhero persona standing in front of you. You can see how powerful and confident they are. They embody everything that is great about you.
>
> Now I want you to step forward into your persona. The two of you become one. You body starts to feel strong and confident, just like the superhero you saw standing in front of you. Hold onto that feeling as you open your eyes and take on whatever you need to get done.

Soar above the Crowd

Not only do you need to step into your persona and have the confidence to really take on the world and let your brilliance shine, but you want to make sure you stand out from the crowd.

Here is a little secret that I want to share with you. One of the best ways to stand out in this crowded marketplace is to be known for something. You see, there are so many people out there simply relying on just being their job title. They are a "business coach" or an "author". They are the ones who just state what they do such as "Virtual Assistant" or "copywriter". Do you want to know the problem with this?

You are lumped in with every other person in your field. You will be compared to every other person with the same job title or who provides the same service. You will be lumped in with the mediocre people who do what you do. However, you can change this by creating your own unique place in the market.

I chose to go full superhero and completely went for it. I made my persona, I put it out there and I owned it. Now when I do anything I just go for it, but I know that some people want to be a little subtler about it and that is ok too.

You can be known for something without going full superhero. In fact you can be known for just about anything, a technique you created, a speciality that you offer or just the type of people you work with. No matter what you choose, you need to make sure you pick something which has room to grow with time and reflects your personality.

We come back to picking what will suit you, not solely where the money is. For example, there were a lot of people that saw there was money to be made by teaching people how to use social media to promote their business.

So, they set out to be an expert in this and they built a name around it. However, after a while the market was flooded with people claiming they could do the same thing, so they had to change what they did. But the problem was, they were known as a social media expert, so they needed to rebrand. This is hard to do and if you change too often you start to lose credibility around what you are doing.

However, if you step up as someone that people are intrigued with, you have room to change directions and fill gaps in the market because people want to learn from you.

They will be fascinated with what you are doing next, they will love your style and they will know what to expect. Think of it like when you are looking for a movie to watch and you have the choice of two films.

One has an actor whose work you enjoy and the other one has good reviews, but you don't know anyone in it. Which one do you pick? Probably the one with the actor you like, because chances are, you will enjoy it. This is the same reason why people will choose to stick with you. They love the work you do, they feel like they're a part of your life and they know, like and trust you.

How do you go about creating a larger than life persona that people want to be around? You be yourself, just a super version of you. You share your life, your thoughts, your work and most of all your personality. You be real, it's not about making stuff up about yourself because people will see through that quickly. It is about being the best version of you that you can be.

This is when you don your cape, step into your super persona and begin to do what you do best, moving forward step by step.

With each day that passes, it gets easier, you become more confident and you own your superhero persona because you just know that it is you. All of you! The best bits, the quirks, the flaws, the passion and the natural abilities. Your smile shines bright, your brilliance is obvious for everyone to see and finally you feel like you have made it!

Don't just take my word for it. Try it out yourself. Nothing beats going out and testing all of this. Pay attention to the people around you and see if you can spot the ones who are embracing their inner superheroes, look for the ones who are being drained every day because they have lost their passion and pay attention to the traits both display. You have those traits too - both the good and the bad. The difference is, you know that you have a choice as to what you want to do with them.

What will that be?

> *"Believe in yourself! Have faith in your abilities! Without a humble but reasonable confidence in your own powers you cannot be successful or happy."*
> **~Norman Vincent Peale**

Exercise: Larger than life presence

What can you do to stand out from the crowd?

What can you be known for?

Make a list of things that will set you apart from the crowd and then make a list of ways you can add that to your marketing.

Cape Flappers

"Sometimes your cape flaps in the wind because you are flying ahead and sometimes because there is someone special behind you flapping it up and down! Either way you are a superhero!!!"
~ Amanda Robins

Sometimes we just need a little extra help. We are so close to our business and our abilities that we lose sight of how great we can be. We forget how far we have come and what wonderful things we are really achieving. We take things personally and to heart, when all we need is an outside perspective.

We can't work in a vacuum. I work from home and most of the time I'm alone. I'm critical of my own work and no matter what I do, I worry that it is not good enough. I see other people's work and I think "Wow, how do they do that?" When it comes to my work, it never seems to match up.

However, when I put it out there and get feedback, people start telling me what they get out of it and it usually is exactly what they wanted. If I didn't do this, I would be sitting there judging my work harshly because it is my work.

I can see the flaws in it, I can see what I wanted it to be and I know that sometimes it doesn't match up to what I imagined. Here's the thing though, the people who it is intended for - they don't see that, they just see it for what it is. If they like it, fantastic, it then becomes good enough for me and if they don't, that's ok too. It just means I need to go back to the drawing board.

Do you ever feel like that? That your work is not good enough? That you just need to add that little bit more? That if you could rewrite it just one more time then it would be perfect?

You are not alone. We all do that. This is when you need your cape flappers the most. They believe in what you have to offer. They can see that you are someone special and they are just waiting for you to catch up and really see how spectacular you are. They are more than happy to flap your cape until you feel that you deserve to fly.

Best of all, you can be a cape flapper too. As you know, we all need a little help with something. You can step up, grab the bottom of someone else's cape and flap away. Why? Because success is contagious! The people who are really confident, those who are really secure in their brilliance know that if you are surrounded by success and you are truly happy for others, then you catch the success bug too. That's right, you too will be successful. The energy of success around you begins to fill you, you begin to see that anything is possible, and you know that you will be supported on your journey.

I once told a dear friend of mine who has believed in me for years that I would never leave her behind and as I began to fly, I made sure that I reached my hand out to grab hers because she is coming with me every step of the way. It is the same for all the people around me. I want to bring them with me and in return they bring more people with them.

We live in a world of abundance, unlimited possibilities and opportunities. There is no reason whatsoever to push people down to build yourself up. We all deserve to fly and we all have the right to own our brilliance. I am honoured to share that journey with you!

Watching From Above

There is a story about a young boy who used to play soccer.

This boy would come each week for regular practice but never made the team - he was always a reserve. Every practice session the boy's father would sit at the far end of the stands and wait for him.

The soccer season started. The young boy didn't show up for practice or for the quarter or semifinals. Then one day the boy turned up for the Grand Final, approached the coach and begged to play. "Coach, you have always left me as a reserve and never let me play. But can you PLEASE let me play today?"

The coach looked at the boy and said "I can't let you play. There are better players than you and this is the Grand Final. I couldn't possibly let you play today".

The boy pleaded again "Coach, I promise I won't let you down. Please give me a chance to play." Eventually the coach gave him a chance despite his better judgment.

The game started and the boy played like a superstar. Every time he got the ball he scored and he stood out as the star of the game.

After the final buzzer sounded, the coach approached the boy and said, "Son, I was so wrong. I have never seen you play like this before. Why have you waited until now to show me that you can really play?"

The boy replied "Coach, my father is watching me today". The Coach looked around but he couldn't see the boy's father anywhere. "Son, I can't see your father here today. I have seen him every week watching you at practice so what makes today so different?"

The boy took a deep breath, wiped away a tear and replied "Coach, there is something I've never told you. My father was blind. Four days ago he died. Today is the first day he could watch me from above".

> **Exercise: Cape Flapping**
>
> Write a list of people who have been behind you, flapping your cape.
>
> Write a list of people who you can help to discover their inner superhero.

Behind Every Great Success

Stephen King's first novel Carrie was rejected from publishers 30 times. Faced with so much rejection, King threw his manuscript in the trash. When his wife Tabitha found his novel in the bin she recovered it and with a genuine belief in his abilities she encouraged him to finish it.

Now Stephen King is a household name selling over 350 million copies of his numerous books, which have also been adapted into countless motion pictures.

It can be a lot to take in. Having permission to be yourself and live up to your real potential can be something that might take a little while to really sink in. Please take the time to really feel into it. I want to leave you with something that I tell all my clients and something that I want to tell you too.

"Let me believe in you until you believe in yourself"

I believe that you are special, I believe that you have something spectacular to offer the world and I will believe in you for as long as it takes for you to believe in yourself! Trust me when I say, you will believe in yourself quicker than you ever thought possible!

Chapter Six

FLY

Chapter Six ~ FLY

Confidence Takes Practice

Many people believe that you either have confidence or you don't. This is simply not true. We all have times when we feel confident and times when we don't. We can also feel confident in some things that we do and less than confident in other things.

No matter where we start, having confidence takes practice. It takes time to build your confidence and it takes mindful effort to not fall for our own hype. To be truly confident we must be grounded in our abilities and humble in our view of ourselves.

You have the ability to achieve great things if you simply believe. The next thing you need to do is prove to yourself that this belief comes from a place where you can deliver. When you can back up your belief, your confidence will grow and you'll FLY.

In the Superfy Universe, when you FLY, you **F**ully **L**ove **Y**ourself!

When you truly feel this, follow your passion and shine your natural brilliance throughout your work, you will also **F**ully **L**ove **Y**our Business!

As you continue using your superpowers, building your confidence and beginning to FLY, remember you are not alone! Just as it takes a whole village to raise a baby and it takes a village to build a successful business.

Your Vibe Attracts Your Tribe

This has been said in so many different ways over the years but however you say it, like attracts like. So whatever you put out into the market place is what you will get back.

For example, if you are feeling stressed, broke and helpless, that is the energy you put out into the world and that is exactly the type of people you will attract into your business. You will attract clients who want to haggle your prices down and complain about everything. They cry poor even after you've helped them so you end up continuing the cycle of misery.

However, if you change your vibe you will attract dream clients who you absolutely love working with. This goes for virtually anything you do. If you are a gossip, you will attract gossips and you better believe they are talking about you just as much as you are talking about them. The genuine and compassionate people who you would rather attract will avoid you because of your negative vibe.

Pick your target market based on their personality traits. That may be different than anything that you have ever come across before but I want to assure you that it makes a massive difference in your business.

For example, you may have been picking your target market based on their age, gender, income, location, interests etc. This is what most business courses tell you to do, however there is a different way.

Try instead to pick who you want to work with based on their personality traits. Why? Just because someone can afford you or fits into your target market doesn't mean you will enjoy working with them. Who would you rather work with?

Someone who pays you but then whines and complains the whole time about how they can't do something? Someone who feels that they paid too much to work with you? Or someone who tells you that they appreciate you and what you do for them? Someone who says thank you for everything that you do, even the tiny things? Someone who shouts from the roof tops about how wonderful you are? I know which ones I work with.

Personally, I have always found the "pick your target market by their demographics" thing very limiting.

Who am I to say that someone can't work with me because they don't fit into a box? As long as they have the personality traits of the people I love to work with, I say bring it on!

Now I want to let you in on a little secret. You can make a list of personality traits of your dream clients but you have to make sure that these traits are also yours. If you want people who don't question your prices, you must be happy to pay your bills, if you want people to be respectful of your time, you must be respectful of other people's time as well.

If you want people to appreciate you then you MUST appreciate others. Be your ideal client and your ideal clients will be drawn to you as if by magic.

> **Exercise: Your Vibe**
>
> Write a list of personality traits of people you would love to work with.
>
> Write a list of qualities of people you don't want to work with.
>
> Go through the two lists and see if there are any qualities on these lists that you are displaying.
>
> Are your qualities on the dream list or the nightmare list?
>
> If they are on the dream list, fantastic!
>
> If they are on the nightmare list, you have some work to do.
>
> Once you have changed your vibe to align with your dream list, burn the nightmare list. You want to make sure you focus on the positive rather than the negative.

Super Sidekicks

As you begin to step into your full power and your business begins to grow fast, you will need to enlist the help of some super sidekicks. These are the people who will help you get the job done and get it done right.

There are a few ways to enlist people to help you. One way is to simply employ them. You will need to outsource quite a lot of the things you would have normally done yourself as you begin to grow. When you are first starting out, you may have had to do everything yourself because you either didn't have the money to employ someone or you have not found people who you trust.

You can attract wonderful people to help you but you may have to kiss a few frogs to find the perfect ones. When you do find them, hold on to them, tell them how much you appreciate them and flap their capes until they too believe in their abilities. Just because you're paying them, doesn't mean you get to act like you own them.

Another way to enlist the help of super sidekicks is by creating joint ventures. There are people out there who are truly talented at what they do. Chances are, they can be the perfect match to put the passion into areas of your business that you hate. Have you ever had a task that drives you crazy, takes 5 times as long as you think it should and that you could quite happily do without, given the chance?

There is someone out there who enjoys doing that job, they can do it super fast and 10 times better than you can. Why not enlist people to help you in your business and then you can do the things you enjoy and that you are super good at.

Exercise: Super Sidekicks

Make a list of things you have to do in your business that you would like to outsource.

Make a list of the qualities of your ideal sidekicks.

Make a list of people who you could team up with to create something amazing.

Make a plan to enlist these sidekicks and make the magic happen.

Superhero Alliance

Wow what a journey it has been to get here! What is one of the biggest things that will really help you release your superhero confidence into the world?

Simple! Surround yourself with other AWESOME superheroes.

The combined powers of people authentically living their lives, going out into the world, helping people and just being themselves – that's a force you have to experience to believe. I have to tell you, I'm hooked.

I had spent so much time in the business world where it was all "compete, compete, compete" and no one really stopped to truly be themselves. You see, all of us, including myself, were putting on this professional image that we thought we needed, in order to make it big in business. It was all a game of smoke and mirrors and it was exhausting. You never really knew who was there to help you and who just wanted to make money from you. You couldn't tell who was really successful and who was bankrupt.

I wanted to live in a world where authentic people were running reputable and genuine businesses. A place where you could escape shoddy business practices. A place where people escaped their limiting beliefs about what was possible.

What is the best way to do this? To surround yourself with other superheroes that feel the same way as you. You can do that by building a super alliance.

Start by connecting with people who are on the same wavelength as you. Surround yourself with knowledge and resources that really speak to you and continue this every day until you really find yourself empowered by the people around you.

This is the main reason why I started the Superfy Alliance. I wanted to create a place where people feel safe to share their ideas, where they would be empowered to follow their dreams and where they could simply be themselves. You can create this for yourself or you are more than welcome to join us.

Surround yourself with people who will encourage you, support you and who will call bullsh*t on you when you start buying into your own hype. It is about more than surrounding yourself with "yes men", It is about finding people who genuinely have your back.

Napoleon Hill talks about this as one of the most powerful tools you can have at your disposal in his book "Think & Grow

Rich". This one principle is my guilty pleasure, one of my keys to success and that is a mastermind group. The answers, insights and guidance you can get from being part of a collective group of likeminded people who all want to see each other succeed is a powerful force that words can't describe. You have to experience it to believe it.

As you become the confident spectacular superhero that I know you are, make sure you surround yourself with other marvellous superheroes that want to help you succeed, just as much as you want to help them!

From Self Employed Psychologist To 'Woman With A Mission' ~ Sallyanne Stone

As a practising psychologist, building self esteem and confidence has been an every day topic with my clients. It has been wonderful to see their growth, however my own growth has often felt like I'm pulling teeth out - with a sledge hammer!

Moving from self employed Psychologist to 'woman with a mission' and creating The Happier Business Project has stretched my self belief and confidence almost to snapping point. I have often had to ask myself, "What advice would I give to a client?", or "What have I learned about this from my clients?"

Knowing what you want to achieve and not being there just yet can be excruciating. Sometimes it's as if the closer you get, the greater the pain – a little like childbirth – that painful final stage of labour just before that amazing gift of your baby.

When we are on the cusp of the success we want, we need toleration for the pain of living on the cusp, and I've decided right in this moment to call this challenge 'cusping'.

It's that almost intolerable place where your desired success is like a cruel person teasing you, holding that sweet treat just beyond arms reach.

Many distant moons ago I ran workshops as a careers counsellor. Participants arrived full of hope, to clarify their career direction. One activity gripped their attention more than any other – and it may resonate with you.

I drew a circle with the word 'Now' and then on the other side of the board a circle with the words 'My Ideal Work' and asked: "What happens when you begin to think about or take steps toward what you want, as you move out of the circle?". Participants responded with "feeling anxious, scared" – occasionally "excited" but usually fear took top spot – then I asked "So what do you think happens for most people when they feel scared?" and they agreed that often we scuttle back to the 'Now' spot, even if it's something we really want and that fits us perfectly.

Now this is an example of cusping – we all need to find ways to keep going. By the way, it wasn't actually clarity that participants needed, they needed personal permission, guts and support to keep moving despite the pain.

How have I managed my own cusping challenges?

Support is the number one key – you must get out of your own head and limited mindset, talk aloud and feed on other's perspectives. Wonderful mentors have been great to talk with about what I want, my fears and doubts, moving beyond 'fliff flaff' thoughts circulating in my head. This 'reframing' brings in freshness, new insights and knocks out unhelpful beliefs. You might notice that the happiest, most successful businesses are not run by a one man/woman show. There is always support – there is no such a thing as synergy with a single person.

That takes us to the second key – *Knock apart unhelpful beliefs*. Your beliefs are self perpetuating, manifesting, sneaky creatures that have the potential to destroy your success. Take heart in the fact that when your thoughts are troubling you, you are probably on the right track. Take time out to learn techniques such as energy psychology and positive mindset psychology to take control. Your limiting thoughts and feelings are like naughty children, so become the mature parent and take control. Many quick and simple techniques work brilliantly.

Making a difference and stepping things up for your business is profoundly challenging at a psychological level – especially for women. I have had to challenge outmoded ideas that suggest that women should be in the background, where the boys are the real 'experts'. Although I am a child of the 70's, women's freedom was slow to really catch on and giving myself permission to 'go public' and be seen and heard has been an almighty challenge. I am immensely relieved that I have tools to deal with that internal mind 'flack' that stops me at times from believing it's ok to speak out loudly and shout my message of value to the masses.

I use mindset techniques with clients but most importantly on myself. So, what difference do they make? I have felt the shift from being overwhelmed to feeling free, motivated and keen to run off, jump and skip ahead.

Whenever I can't get moving, I am self doubting or doubting my vision, I have literally lost that breath of fresh air -*Inspiration. This is the most important key.* When inspiration is there, I know I am on the right track, I can feel that rightness down to the blood and bones of my body. It's exciting and it's about having reconnected with the truth of who I am, what is profoundly meaningful, and the vision that I know with 100 % confidence will make a difference and is perhaps my calling and even destiny. This gives what I do the 'wow' factor. Funnily enough, it coincides with my ego stepping aside, it's no longer about little 'ol Sallyanne but something much more important.

I believe you have a calling, something that is profoundly, uniquely you. My advice is to seek that out, speak to people about it, test the waters, claim your voice and shout out your message in whatever you do. That will be your greatest source of confidence – and you are worth it – 100%.

SALLYANNE'S BIO

Sallyanne Stone is the founder of The Happier Business Project. The Project's mission is to share happier mindset secrets that lead to freedom and success for small business owners.

Sallyanne's passion for helping people builds on her professional training and thousands of hours working in career coaching, rehabilitation, and consulting as a Psychologist.

A client once suggested that she 'bottle up' her knowledge and share her skills further afield, hence Sallyanne now brings her expertise to the small business community.

These powerful techniques work quickly and are backed by clinical research. Happiness and personal freedom is the starting point to achieve business success.

If you have a happier business story to inspire others, or want to achieve a happier pathway to business success, you can download Sallyanne's Quick Start Guide right now or email Sallyanne Stone at *www.thehappierbusinessproject.com.au*.

Exercise: Superhero Alliance

Who can you align yourself with, to increase your power?

Make a list of the qualities of the people you can surround yourself with that will help you FLY!

Chapter Seven

Putting It All Together

Chapter Seven ~Putting It All Together

Now Comes The Fun Part!

Firstly, congratulations for getting this far in the book. I know personally it is a pretty big achievement to get to the last chapter of a book. There was a study conducted that showed that only 5% of people actually read a book all the way to the end. You are just a few short pages away from being one of these elite people!

I hope you can now see that YOU ARE A SUPERHERO! You are spectacular and you have new and exciting ways to release the superhero confidence that is locked up inside you.

As you read through the book there were many exercises designed to create awareness and give you a kick start to unleashing your inner superhero. Let's go through them and see how they will help you really FLY!

Even the smallest things will make a big difference not only to you but to anyone you are able to help.

The Little Things Matter

An old man walking along a beach at dawn noticed a young man ahead of him picking up starfish and flinging them into the sea. Catching up with him, he asked what he was doing. "The starfish will die if they are still on the beach when the sun roasts them with its mid-morning heat," came the answer. "But the beach goes on for miles, and there are millions of starfish," countered the old man. "How can your effort make any difference?" The young man looked at the starfish in his hand and threw it safely into the waves. "It makes a difference to this one," he said.

Putting the Superhero Confidence Formula Into Action

Are you ready to discover your superpowers?

Ego Check~ Once you have made sure you are coming from a genuinely confident place and NOT being directed by your ego, you will be able to make smart choices and succeed in ways you never thought possible.

Reconnect With Your Inner Child ~ Now it is time to enjoy yourself and really begin to dream again. Spend time each day using your imagination to create an image in your mind of the future you deserve.

Uncover Your Origin Story ~ Once you have written your origin story, introduce it into your marketing. If you have a very detailed origin story, you don't want to put it out there all at once. It can be quite overwhelming for some people. It is like when you meet someone for the first time and they begin to tell you everything about their life starting from childhood. What you do is share your story in parts. Use the bits that are most relevant to the people you are connecting with at the time. Just make sure your story is consistent and real because they will remember the things you said and if they don't match up then all your credibility goes out the window.

Your BIG Dream ~ Now you have your big dreams somewhere that you can see them, it is time to take steps forward and allow the universe to deliver. If you dream small, you'll achieve small but if you dream BIG, you'll achieve BIG!

Step One: Escaping the Ordinary

Greatness List ~ You've put it out there now, good for you! You are meant to be GREAT and do amazing things. All you need to do now is take one baby step at a time to achieve your destiny.

Cutting Off The Ball And Chain ~ Are you feeling lighter and free to FLY, now you have cut off the ball and chain holding you down? You will come across this again and again as you move forward in your success but always remember you have a choice.

Getting Started ~ Just one step forward, one email, one Facebook post, anything in the direction of getting started is such a big thing. It may not feel like much but it will lead to the next little thing and then the next until you have created the momentum of a runaway train.

Step One: Escaping the Ordinary

Identify Your Inner Super Hero ~ Are you excited to identify your inner superhero? I'm excited for you! Whether you show off your inner superhero to the public or keep it secret, you can tap into your power any time you need.

Your Inner Critic ~ Your inner critic just wants to be heard and understood. Every day you communicate with your inner critic the easier it will be for the two of you to work together to achieve your dreams.

Understanding The Haters ~ You'll be faced with people who will say things that can take you back a few steps. When you come across things like this, stand back, look for the reasons why and face the situation with kindness and understanding.

Your Cheer Squad ~ Do you have a cheer squad? I bet you do! Make sure you tell them that you appreciate them for believing in you, it will mean more than you think. If you don't, you're welcome to come and join mine.

Unique You ~ You're unique and special. Can you see that now? I can see it in you. Now take all your quirks and special traits and turn them into assets in everything you do.

Your Natural Abilities~ Once you have begun to dig into your natural abilities and started to use them, it feels fantastic. Opportunities to help people and build your dream business will begin to come to you as if from nowhere.

Step Three: Training your Superpowers

Circle of Excellence ~ How does it feel to be filled with confidence? Take your circle with you wherever you go and you will soon be able to FLY no matter what you are doing.

Fake It Until You Make It ~ Soon you will not have to fake your confidence because you will be faced with overwhelming evidence of just how spectacular you are.

Kryptonite To Power ~ Flaws don't have to be your kryptonite; you can turn them into positives, one little step at a time. Remember to own your flaws, address the elephant in the room and use them to create a connection with your tribe.

Archnemesis ~ Remember that it is only you that can give your power away. Hold your head up high, rise above the challenges and keep your power strong by living with integrity.

Creating magic ~ Once you have a list of products or services you can offer, get out there and start creating them. Too many people get stuck creating something all alone thinking that it has to be done perfectly before they can present it or even sell it but it doesn't have to be this way. There is no energy doing it all by yourself. Find people you trust, that you can test your products or services on, to see if you are on the right track. You will be amazed that what you thought people wanted and what they actually want is often quite different.

Getting Knocked Down ~ If you get knocked down, just get up one more time and you will be successful!

Step Four: Don your Cape

Step Into Your Persona ~ Each and every day, step into your persona until it truly feels like a part of you.

Larger than life presence ~ Once you know what you want to be known for, simply repeat it over and over again until people begin to repeat it back to you and then repeat it again to yourself. Strategy, consistency and repetition are the keys to being remembered. Go out and make your larger than life presence felt.

Cape Flapping ~ Thank your cape flappers and repay them by either returning the favour or paying it forward. The more superheroes we can unleash on the world, the better it will be.

Step Five: FLY

Your Vibe ~ Continue to pay attention to the vibe you are putting out. One of the best ways to see what you are putting out into the world is to pay attention to what you are getting back. If you are getting complainers, take a look at what you are complaining about. If you are attracting the right people, continue doing what you are doing. Awareness is the key.

Super Sidekicks ~ Build your team one super sidekick at a time. Look for quality, treat them with respect and make sure you are offering win-win opportunities for everyone involved.

Superhero Alliance ~ Surround yourself with success and you will be successful. Give as much as you receive. If you are surrounded with people with a poverty mindset you will soon have a poverty mindset too. But if you surround yourself with people who have a prosperity mindset, you too will have a prosperity mindset.

"I Just Needed An Epic Failure to Spur Me On...." ~ Con Dolmas

When I was 15, the Managing Director of McDonalds Australia told me that if I wanted to take charge of a major corporation one day, and play a significant role in shaping its future, then I should become an accountant.

Well, he didn't exactly say it like that, but that's the message I took away that day.

So I became an accountant.

The only problem was that I never really loved working with numbers.

What I loved was working with people.

And what I loved most, was helping people transform themselves by acquiring new skills.

So I guess you could say a role as a trainer and coach was a natural fit.

It should have been obvious to everyone, especially me, that this is where I belonged.

But unfortunately, it's the obvious that we often have trouble recognizing within ourselves, and for me the obvious was recognizing my affinity with training and my expertise as a trainer and a coach.

I waited around for someone else to 'legitimize' what I knew deep down, was my unspoken truth. That I was in fact, damn good at teaching ordinary people how to do extraordinary things.

I was waiting around for somebody else to "anoint me" as a coach, as a trainer.....as an expert.

I was waiting around for somebody else to legitimize my expertise and recognize my ability to help others by giving me an "official title"....

A title that would secretly allow me to believe that I was good enough to be recognized as an expert and to teach others valuable skills that would ultimately help them improve their lives.

In the end, I didn't actually need a title to give me the confidence to come out as a 'legitimate' expert.

I just needed an epic failure to spur me on....

And I got one.

It was 2007 and I was working as an organizational change manager for one of Australia's most iconic multinational corporations.

At the time I was part of a project team rolling out a massive financial system across four continents.

As part of that rollout, we were implementing a new tech support team, and had set up a help desk and a telephone helpline so that staff could contact the support team if they had a problem.

You know what it's like, the budget was tight, so rather than spend money on hiring professionals to record our telephone support messages, we ran an internal competition to crown one "lucky" staff member as "The Voice" of the Finance Help Desk and have him or her record all the phone messages.

Staff entered the competition by calling an internal phone number and leaving a message on the voicemail.

At the end of the competition, a judging panel was convened, and a handful of managers listened to the recordings and chose the winner.

I wasn't on the judging panel, so I was free to submit my entry. So that's exactly what I did.

Picture this.

There I am practicing my little heart out.

I'm doing my very best impersonation of a "slick, deep and bombastic radio announcer voice" and as I'm listening to the sound of my own voice I'm thinking....wow....I sound so slick and polished...... I'm a shoe in...... I've got this crown nailed.

In hindsight, what I thought sounded "slick" was just so inauthentic that it was horrible....it sounded so fake and disengaging....there was no real meaning being communicated....it was just a guy trying to sound like somebody else.

Ultimately there was nothing authentic in what came out of my mouth.

But at the time I thought it was magnificent because over the years, my ear had been tuned to FM radio and my idea of what a "good voice" sounded like was this big bombastic radio announcer voice.

So it was time for the judges to announce a winner.

I'm thinking I'm a shoe in... nobody who entered the competition sounds as deep and bombastic as me.

But you know what?

I didn't even come close...

A friend of mine got the role and when I heard what she had recorded, I remember thinking at the time, I can't tell you why I liked hers more than I liked mine, but I just did.....

I thought to myself, I don't know what she's got, I don't know how she did it but she instinctively understood how to make it sound engaging and authentic....it just really drew you in.

And so whilst her recording really drew you in, mine had the opposite effect.

It was an epic failure.

And so I too felt like an epic failure.

So I decided right there and then that I was going to learn how to do this voice stuff properly because I never wanted to feel that low again.

I never again wanted to be the guy who thought he'd nailed it, only to find out how crap he really was.

So I went straight to the top and enrolled in Australia's National Institute of Dramatic Art (NIDA) to learn the art and science of voice over.

As fate would have it, one of my instructors turned out to be one of Australia's most prolific big brand voice over artists.

You can switch on the radio and television in Australia, wait a few minutes and chances are you'll hear his voice, I mean, his voice is everywhere.

Now he was one of the instructors at this course and we kind of clicked.

So much so that when the opportunity presented itself to be coached by him one-on-one in his personal recording studio, I jumped on board.

I used to think it was all about how my voice sounded, and I didn't really even think about the message I was truly conveying.

I spent the next few years studying voice-over & communication techniques with my new mentor, learning the art and science of using voice to communicate meaning in a way that truly engages the listener.

And almost a decade down the track, I'm still a student of voice and communication. I'm also a voice over artist and communication coach in my own right, a recognized expert in this domain, and my voice has been heard on corporate training and business communications for some rather well known brands including Microsoft, Vodafone, Telstra, LG, ANZ Bank, NRMA, Symantec & Novartis Pharmaceuticals.

Today I easily slip on my "expert" cape and feel confident enough to acknowledge my own expertise.

Why?

Because I don't need anybody else to bestow upon me a label or a title to know that when I share my lifetime of learning with other people, they can achieve extraordinary, often transformational results.

And just being able to see the same level of enthusiasm and competency in the people that I help, the same high that I felt when I first "got it right" (whatever "it" may be), that's actually worth more to me than any title or external recognition.

That's what nurtures my inner superhero.

Every day, you and I learn something new, whether it's something in our professional lives, or even in our personal lives.

Some choose to take that learning, reinforce it through action and then help others do the same thing.

These people transition from being a "Doer" to a "Sharer" to a "Teacher", and in doing so, help more people begin their own transition.

Imagine what this little planet of ours could achieve if we all traversed this path.

CON'S BIO

Con Dolmas is an international expert in the field of Voiceover for Corporate Training, Business Communications and eLearning.

He helps online trainers and video marketers instantly transform their voice to sound engaging, confident and professional.

Con reckons he helps his clients find their authentic voice. His clients just reckon that Con makes them sound great.

As the creator of The Narration Navigator method, a simple and effective 5-step system that helps online trainers record their own powerfully engaging audio, and the author of "Voice Over for eLearning – the Essential Introduction for Online Trainers", Con is helping to change the nature of online audio in the 21st Century.

With almost a decade of experience in corporate training narration for large organizations including Microsoft, Vodafone, ANZ Bank, NRMA, AAP Telecommunications, Leighton Contractors and Novartis Pharmaceutical, plus over 15 years of professional business services experience working with a diverse range of high-profile organizations including QANTAS Airlines, Unisys Corporation, Optus, Vodafone and Kelloggs, Con has a strong track record of achievement in business.

To discover more, go to www.ConDolmas.com

Final Thoughts

The first step to achieving anything is awareness. There is a lot to take in throughout this book and it is all designed to open up your awareness so that when you are faced with situations that can help you or harm you, you know that you have a choice.

I can't express in the words in this book just how ahhh-mazing you really are! If only I could hold up a mirror for you to see what spectacular abilities you possess!

Embrace who you really are and surround yourself with other authentic superheroes. These are the people you want to fill your life with because they will be the ones who will hold your hand and take you with them as they FLY.

Your tribe is out there just waiting for you to offer them a way to work with you. All you need to do is don your cape, step into the role you were born to take and use your superpowers to change lives, one step at a time!

Meet Amanda

Amanda Robins aka Brainstorm is the go-to Intuitive Creative Director teaching you how to harness the power of visual storytelling, so you can creatively plan, embrace plot twists and influence the outcomes in your life, career and business.

She has a unique perspective on how our minds work, understanding the story we are telling the world and pinpointing the little changes we can make that can instantly have an impact.

With the vision to build an authentic community of everyday heroes working together to live above the ordinary by overcoming feelings of unworthiness, extreme doubt, and generations of limiting beliefs to create long-lasting change by using their imagination and creativity.

Happy to openly share her years of knowledge as a former food addict, intuitive creative director, marketer, 6-time international best-selling Amazon author, business owner, entrepreneur, trainer, speaker, loving mother and superhero, Amanda is able to answer questions with the reassurance that the advice given is backed by actual experience.

**The PAST is your ORIGIN story,
The PRESENT is your POWER and
The FUTURE is waiting for you to WRITE it!**

Are you ready for the adventure to begin?

Visit http://www.askbrainstorm.com/ to start your journey

today!

www.ingramcontent.com/pod-product-compliance
Lightning Source LLC
LaVergne TN
LVHW051608070426
835507LV00021B/2831